Stock options for beginners

Find out what stock options are and learn how to trade them effectively

DAVE GREENE

Copyright © Dave Greene 2020, all rights reserved.

Table Of Contents

Introduction	vi
Chapter One	1
What Are Stock Options	1
MONEY TERMS: ASSETS, SECURITY AND STOCKS	2
WHAT ARE OPTIONS?	5
WHAT ARE STOCK OPTIONS?	6
HOW STOCK OPTIONS WORK	7
THE BASICS OF STOCK OPTIONS: CALLS, PUTS & PREMIUM	9
FACTORS AFFECTING THE PREMIUM	18
OPTION VALUATION MODELS	19
STOCK OPTION TRADING	23
HOW STOCK OPTIONS ARE TAXED	25
Chapter two	1
The Good And The Bad	1
THE UPSIDES OF A STOCK OPTIONS	3
THE DOWNSIDES OF AN OPTION	10
Chapter three	18
Evolution Of Stock Options	18
THE BEGINNING	18
17TH CENTURY: THE TULIP MANIA	20
18TH CENTURY	25

19TH CENTURY: RUSSELL SAGE AND OVER THE COUNTER TRADE OPTIONS 25

20TH CENTURY: THE TURNING POINT 27

THE FUTURE OF STOCK OPTIONS 31

    CHAPTER FOUR 33
    EMPLOYEE STOCK OPTIONS 33

UNDERSTANDING EMPLOYEE STOCK OPTIONS 36

WHAT YOU CAN DO WITH YOUR ESOS 41

DRAWBACKS OF EXCHANGE-TRADED OPTIONS 43

ESO VS OTHER COMPENSATIONS 46

HOW TO DEAL ESOS 49

ESO HEDGING STRATEGIES 51

    CHAPTER FIVE 55
    GETTING UP TO SPEED 55

YOU ARE ON YOUR OWN 55

UNDERSTANDING THE STOCK OPTION QUOTES 56

HOW TO CHOOSE AN OPTION TRADING PLATFORM 69

    CHAPTER SIX 73
    BASIC OPTION STRATEGIES 73
    CHAPTER SEVEN 83
    ADVANCED OPTION STRATEGIES 83
    REFERENCES 97

Introduction

The sky is the limit in the world of investment. There are basically unlimited opportunities available to everyone with many more coming up daily. Back in the days, investment was limited to stocks, bonds, venture capitalism, and a few others.

Over the years, new opportunities have crept into the mainstream and they kept coming up at an alarming rate. Now we have mutual funds, equity funds, index funds, futures, forex, cryptocurrency, and options trading among several others.

While this growth and increased opportunities look and sound good, it's at the cost of simplicity. As a newbie to investment, knowing which opportunity to decide on can be a nightmare.

What if you chose the wrong opportunity? What if you lose all your money? Which one is the best one? Which one is the worst one?

Many questions like these besiege every newbie.

In truth, every investment opportunity has its ups and downs. There is not a single investment opportunity that is all good or that is all bad. They each operate under certain conditions and they have their particular risks associated with them. The reasonable decision is to have a good understanding of each opportunity before delving into it.

It's a poor strategy to try out an investment opportunity when you don't fully understand how it works and the dangers associated with it.

Remedying this is precisely what this book is about.

This book is about a single investment opportunity: Stock options trading. It's a comprehensive guide that teaches a beginner what stock options trading is, how it works, the risks, and how to profit from it.

For you to be reading this, you have definitely considered investing in stock options. But stock options probably look too sophisticated or ambiguous for you. Therefore, you decided to read a book about it. There is that feeling with every new investor.

There will always be those myths that only the selected few ever make a profit on options. That options are a shady trade similar to playing the casino, and that it's nigh impossible to figure out correctly.

This book strives to nullify all these myths by presenting options in an easily understood manner. In seven well-written, highly researched, and comprehensive chapters, you will learn virtually everything a newbie stock options trader is required to know.

You will learn how stock options came to be, how it's different from stocks, and what trading looks like. You'll learn that stock options are very flexible investment tools, even more, flexible than stocks.

However, this isn't a motivational book. You'll also learn how options work in the real world: how an average trader uses it and how a company uses it and all the downside associated with its use.

Most importantly, you'll learn how to manage your expectations because more often than not, options are a very risky business. Now that you know what you are in for, let us get into it right away by examining what options are in the next chapter.

Chapter One
What Are Stock Options

One of the investment opportunities introduced to anyone interested in investment is stock options. They are almost as popular as stocks themselves (Amazon, Apple, etc.), if not more. And they can be found on almost all the exchanges you'll find stocks.

The reason stock options are so popular is the wide range of flexibility they offer to investors and companies. Investors don't get as much flexibility as they do in options in trading stocks.

However, a term being popular doesn't always mean simple. To most people, the term "stock options" is often as puzzling as it sounds. Average people find it too difficult to comprehend. Even big companies often end up offering the wrong stock option plans to their employees.

At the end of the day, millions of employees are unable to take full advantage of the options offered to them. In reality, millions of dollars in stock options go to waste yearly. And most of these losses are due to bad decisions on the part of the employees.

The problem doesn't stop there either. For fresh traders looking for a sensational investment opportunity, the world of stock options trading can be intimidating. There are so many insider jargons, corporate terms, agreements, and rules regarding trading options; it can give anyone an awful headache.

The worst of it is that you are expected to be familiar with all the terms before trading. For example, do you know how to carry out an Iron Condor?

I don't think so.

Situations like this make stock options look difficult. At first glance, understanding stock options trading looks like a herculean task.

However, it doesn't have to be. Stock options can be easily understood with the proper tutelage. And that which leads us with a very important question: What are stock options and how do they work?

To answer this in the best and most comprehensive way. We have to go to the basics of finance and investment.

Money Terms: Assets, Security and Stocks

To get a good grasp of what stock options are about. You have to be familiar with the following terms: assets, security, and stocks. They are everyday terms, but how much do you really understand them.

1. Assets

Assets refer to all the resources that have a monetary value to a company or economic entity. They can be used as a revenue source either currently or in the future. The assets of an economic entity represent all the entire value of ownership that can be converted to cash.

Assets take many forms including land, inventory, investments, cash, and so on. The balance sheet of every firm records all the monetary value of that particular firm's assets. Once an asset is used up or sold, it is moved from the balance sheet to the section of the income statement called "expenditures."

In finance and accounting, there are several classifications of assets based on several variables. However, the classification we are most interested in that based on physical presence.

Regarding this, there are two main classes of assets:

a) Tangible Assets
b) Intangible Assets

Tangible assets are assets that are physically present. People can see and touch these physically. Tangible assets include current assets such as inventory and fixed assets such as buildings. Some tangible assets are susceptible to depreciation while others are not.

On the other hand, intangible assets can not be physically felt. They are basic ideas and rights that give every firm a physical presence and power in the marketplace. Intangible assets include trademarks, copyrights, patents, and financial assets such as bonds, accounted receivable, and stocks.

2. Security

Securities are financial instruments, most often intangible financial assets that can be traded for cash. There are many rules dictating the nature of every security and these depend on the jurisdiction of the underlying assets being traded.

In the United States, the term "Security" covers every traded financial asset. These can be broken down into 3 categories.

- a) Debt securities
- b) Equity securities
- c) Derivatives

A debt security is basically borrowed money. They are issued by one party to the other and sold to another at a certain price, with the agreement of payback plus a fixed interest. Examples include bonds and treasury notes.

Equity securities are the stakes of ownership of a business. It refers to the stocks and shares of ownership of the business. Stocks prices rise and fall according to the company's fortunes in the financial markets. Equity securities produce regular earnings in the form of dividends.

Derivatives, on the other hand, are a unique type of security that has its own value linked to an underlying asset. The underlying asset can later be purchased or sold with all the transaction details specified at the initial transaction. The most popular derivatives are futures, mortgage securities, and options. The later is what this book is all about.

So back to our question.

What are Options?

The simplest term for an option is a wager. An option is a dated financial contract between two parties. The contract provides the buyer of the option the right but not the obligation to purchase or sell an underlying asset at a fixed price at or before the contract expiry date. The underlying assets may be stocks, bonds, physical commodities, or even mutual funds.

All options have an expiry date. Prior to the expiry date, the buyer has a fixed period of time to make a decision. The buyer can choose either to buy or sell the underlying asset assigned to the option, sell the option, or let it expire.

Because options are derivative securities, they have lesser worth compared to equities. They only offer traders a chance to make or lose money, in regard to what happens in the future versus their own prediction. This is the broad term of how options trading works. Let's go a step further.

What are Stock Options?

Stock options are the type of options traded only in stocks. They are contracts that offer the investor the freedom but not the obligation—to buy or sell the underlying stocks at a predetermined price for a specified amount of time.

There are two main types of stock options:

a) Call option(a wager that the stock price rises)
b) Put options(a wager that the stock prices falls)

A call option gives the buyer of that option the right to buy a specified amount of stock at an agreed-upon price in the near future. A put option gives the buyer of the option the right to sell a specified amount of stocks at the agreed-upon price in the near future. The money the investor pays to obtain either of these two options is known as the premium.

Stock options are incredibly powerful financial items for all the right reasons. They can enhance your portfolio. They do this because of their versatility. With stock options, as you'll come to realize—there is always a selection that fits an investor's goal.

Investors can make money with any form of speculation with stock options. Therefore, stock options can be used to amass a fortune from a skyrocketing stock or to limit losses from a declining one or to make a profit from a stagnating stock. Stock options can, therefore, offer recurring income, protection, as well as leverage to your portfolio.

However, as it's popularly said, "With great opportunity comes great risk." There is considerable risk in dealing with stock options. If you trade options wrongly, you can end up losing a lot of money. But even with the risk, stock options trading offers invaluable investment opportunities you can't find elsewhere.

How Stock options work

In order for a stock option trade to go through, there have to be two willing parties. These are:

a) Options Buyers or Holders
b) Options Sellers or writers

Those who purchase options are known as the "options holders." They are not obligated to buy or sell. They have the choice to fulfill the terms of their options at any time of their choosing. Doing this is known as exercising the option. Let's say you speculated that Netflix stock price will rise above $470 in the next three months. You went ahead to buy 5 call options that grant you access to purchase five hundred Netflix stocks at $470 anytime in the next three months.

If the three month goes by and the stock price never rises beyond $470. It makes zero financial sense to buy below $470. The good news is that you are not obligated to buy the stocks. You can simply let the stock option contract expire. The option is said to be worthless in this case. Eventually, you will only lose the money you paid to get the option: the premium.

If the stock price rises to an attractive $483 however, you are in luck. You get to purchase 500 shares at a discount price of $470.

The same scenario goes for the trader who buys a put. If the market goes the wrong way, the trader is not obligated to sell. The trader only loses the premium. If the trader predicted directly, however, the trader gets to sell at an attractive price.

Being a writer of an option is where significant risks come in. Those who write options are known as "option sellers." They are expected to buy or sell the stocks if the holder exercises his or her rights. They are expected to make good on the terms of the contract. So, writers can end up losing more money than the premium they received.

Basically, there are four things you can do with a stock option in options trading.

1) Buy calls
2) Buy puts
3) Sell puts
4) Sell calls

As an options trader, you can choose to be on either side of the trade, even at the same time. You can buy options and pay a premium to a seller. You also can write options and receive a premium from prospective buyers. It all depends on your forecast, the strategy you are using, and how much risk you are willing to take on.

When you buy a stock, you have a long position on that stock. Buying a call gives you a potential long position on the underlying stock. Similarly, when you buy a put, the put option gives you a potential short position on the underlying stock.

Meanwhile selling a call places you in a potential short position on the stock, since you can be forced to sell them. Similarly, selling a put gives you a potential long position on the stocks because you might be forced into buying them.

The Basics of Stock Options: Calls, Puts & Premium

As explained above. A Stock option is a contract between two willing parties. A single stock option contract represents 100 shares of the underlying stock.

Because stock options are derivative securities, they grant only the right to purchase, not the obligation or benefits associated with owning a stock. Purchasing an option is like making a down payment for future endeavors.

If you were to buy one call contract of Sony's share, you would have the right to buy 100 shares of Sony of the agreed-upon price. Because a contract represents 100 underlying shares, the premium is the price of the option multiplied by 100.

This agreed-upon price on which the option is exercised is known as the Strike price. The strike prices of options vary, and it has a direct effect on the premium price.

Regarding the premium, it starts with the Bid and Ask price. This Bid price is the price the buyer is willing to pay, while the Ask price is the price the seller is willing to accept. A lot of negotiations go into stock options trading.

The price both parties eventually agree upon is the option price. The option price(T) multiplied by 100 multiplied by the number of contracts(N) purchased equals the premium(P).

$$P = T \times 100 \times N$$

Now, let's explain in detail the three big terms of Stock options.

1. Calls

Imagine you are a quiet suburban homeowner in the United States. Early this year, you noticed increased development in an industrial area next to where you live. The electric car company, Tesla is constructing a huge factory next to other huge upcoming factories owned by the likes of Amazon, Nvidia, and Intel.

A friend of yours who is a real estate agent informs you that over 10 thousand apartment units around the industrial zone belong to one real estate group: Camden property trust.

You predicted that with the boom these businesses will be bringing—real estate prices of these apartments will certainly go up within two years. Therefore, investing in this company looks very promising.

However, rather than buying shares of Camden property trust from the stock market. Your financial advisor advises you to invest in stock options instead.

Let's say at the present moment, Camden stock price trades at $89 per share. You are predicting that can it will go above $95 within two years. So you bought five Camden calls with a strike price of $90 at $5 each. This option will cost you a premium of $2500.

Buying this call means the call writer is wagering against you and hoping that the stock price will stay below $90 at expiry. His aim is to make a profit of the premium you paid.

$$P = 5 \times 100 \times 5 = \$2500$$

If the stock price goes above $90 dollars anytime in the next two years, you'll be able to buy 500 shares at $90 per share regardless of the stock price at that time. If it goes as high as $120, you can still buy them for $90.

When you start trading, you'll start hearing terms like "in-the-money" and "out-of-the-money."

For a call, if the strike price is below the current market price of the stock, it is said to be "in-the-money." If you were to buy a Camden call of $85 when the current market price is $89. You can simply exercise your option the following day and make a profit of $400(89-85x100).

This is not taking into account the premium you paid, taxes, and commissions. It's impossible to make instant money with in-the-money options because they are very expensive.

However, if you were to buy the Camden call at any strike price above the current $89. The option is said to be out of the money. If you bought it at $89, it is said to be "at the money." The option price rises the more in the money it is and falls the more out of the money it is.

Back to our hypothetical discussion. You have purchased 5 out of the money Camden calls. If the stock price fails to rise significantly above $90. You'll have to let the option expire worthless because buying the stocks below the strike price will lead to additional losses.

There is absolutely no point in doing this. The only choice available is to let the option expire worthlessly.

Mind you, to make a profit on the call: the market price needs to rise above the sum of both the strike price and the premium you paid. To make a profit on your Camden call, the market price of the Camden stock needs to rise above $95(90+5).

If the investor in you turns out to be right. And the stock rises to $105 in eighteen months, you can exercise your option and make a steady profit of $5000.

Your down payment of $2500 gives you the right to buy five hundred Camden shares now worth $105 at $90 per share. The writer of the option has no option but to sell the shares to you at the strike price. The instant profit you get to make on exercise is $5000 minus the commission and other charges.

$$Profit = (105-[90+5]) \times 500 = \$5000$$

How calls are exercised

There are basically three ways you can exercise your call namely:

a) Cash exercise

b) Cashless exercise

c) Cashless hold

The most popular method is cash exercise. In this scenario, as the trader, you will come up with the money to purchase the shares you want to exercise. After purchasing the shares, you can then sell them off at the market price to make your profit or you can keep the shares and hope they keep rising.

The cashless exercise allows you to purchase the shares on credit and pays back the credit after the shares are sold immediately at a higher price on the market. The trader gets to keep the profit as cash.

The last available exercise method is the cashless hold. In this case, the right amount of shares will be sold to cover the cost of purchase. Then, the trader gets to keep the rest of the shares and hope it rises before it's sold.

2. Puts

The best way to think of a put is as an insurance policy. But before we go to the next hypothetical scenario. It's possible to trade with a put in the scenario above.

However, in this instance, you would be the writer of the put, not the holder. If you firmly believe that Camden stock will never dip below $85, you can write a put for that stock and get paid a premium.

The only downside is that if your prediction falls short and, at any time before the expiry, the stock price goes below $85. You would be obligated to buy those shares from the option holder even if the shares are worth zero on the market.

Therefore, your loss as a put seller can be catastrophic. But on the other hand, if your prediction turns out to be correct. You get to keep the premium.

Investors use puts mainly as an insurance policy or as part of their investment strategy. Therefore, puts are not as common as calls. But that doesn't stop us from trying to understand them.

If you noticed that Intel just lost their genius of a CEO to Samsung, and are subsequently making a couple of poor investments. You can go ahead to buy a put for the Intel's stocks you already own. Assuming Intel's current stock price is $60 dollars. You can buy 5 put at $3 each with a strike price of $58.

This strike price for a put is said to be "out-of-the-money" because the current market price of the stock is above it. However, if another put had a strike price above

$60, it would be said to be "in-the-money." Any put at $60 will be at-the-money. The premium paid for the 5 contracts will be $1500.

$$P = 3 \times 100 \times 5 = 1500$$

To make a profit with this put, Intel stocks need to go below $55(58-3) and not just the strike of $58. Let's say the price went down to $48 a month before expiry. If you exercised your option at that moment, you sell off the shares at the rate of $58 dollars to the seller of the option.

This way, you would have enough money to buy back an equal amount of shares, get back the sum of your premium as profit, and still have some gain as leftovers.

On the other hand, if you guessed wrong and the stock price failed to go below $58 before the expiry date. You would have to forfeit the premium to the seller.

3. Option Premium

As you can see, stock options are powerful investment instruments for investors that make the right prediction. At first glance, it looks complex and baffling. But, with the explanations above, I hope you can see it is quite simple once you understand the risks.

Investing in stock options is about predicting the future fortune of a stock and making a wager on it. But this wager is not free. The price of the wager is the premium that is paid to the seller.

And this premium isn't just any price the seller comes up with. All premiums have a calculated market price that fluctuates in accordance with several variables.

Calculating an option premium can be very complex—especially for a beginner like you. This is due to the numerous variables that need to be factored into the calculations.

Nevertheless, there is no harm in covering the basics. Every option premium price is based on 3 components. You have to understand these components to fully grasp how a premium works. The components are:

1) The intrinsic value
2) The time value
3) The implied volatility

The intrinsic value of an option is the difference between the price of the underlying stock and the strike price. If the stock price of an asset trades at $80 on the market and you bought the call at a strike price of $75, the intrinsic value is said to be $5(80-75). This is the reason in-the-money options are infinitely more costly compared to out-of-the-money options.

The time value is related to the duration of the contract and edges closer to zero as the option nears its expiry date. An option that grants you a duration of one month to exercise will be substantially cheaper than one that grants you a year. This is because the chances are more in your side within a year compared to within a month.

Implied volatility is a little bit complex. It is calculated by reviewing the price of the underlying stock, its performance in the past, and the general opinion of the market on its future. It is the variable that accounts for how volatile a stock price might be in the future.

Implied volatility affects the extrinsic value of the option premiums. The higher the volatility of the underlying stock, the more the likelihood of the option finishing in the money. Thus, options with higher implied volatility are more expensive compared to those with lower implied volatility.

Factors affecting the Premium

These three components in regard to the stock price of the underlying asset dictate the price of the premium. Stocks are generally more valuable than each other. The option premium for Intel's stocks trading at $60 on the market will be different from that of Netflix that's trading at $470. The price of the options of each of these stocks will also vary from time to time. This variation will be based on their performance of the stocks on the market. As the stocks become more valuable, so does the option and vice versa.

The intrinsic value is the difference between the current stock price and the strike price. It is the profit you have to gain if you exercised the option today. Therefore, the more in the money an option is, the more intrinsic value the option has. The more out of money it is, the less intrinsic value it has.

Generally, out of the money options have an intrinsic value of zero. Say you bought an Intel's call at a strike price $62. The intrinsic value of that option should be -$2(60-62=-2). But because the value of options can't be negative, the value is said to be zero.

Time value is essentially the amount of time the seller places himself at a risk. The longer the option has to expire, the higher the time value. If the time value of the Apple option for the month of January is 0.8$ per option, you can expect the time value for 6 months to be around $8 per option.

Option Valuation Models

These variables above cover the theoretical idea of how options are priced. In reality, stock options markets employ the use of several mathematical models to calculate their option prices. These models are really complex and they involve serious mathematics and accounting. The good news is that you don't have to learn them.

Many markets and traders have preprogrammed calculators that can help you to determine any option you want to sell. You can also contact your financial advisers for additional information on these.

The most commonly used models are the Black-Scholes Model, Binomial Option Pricing, and the Monte-Carlo simulation. As an investor, you can use these to calculate the range the price of your options will fall in.

The real trade prices of stock options are determined in the open markets. Often times, the real price differs from the theoretical price, but only slightly.

However, knowing the theoretical prices remains a good thing, as they are always close to the real price. Making use of these models allows you to speculate on options and plan your investment strategy.

But before we discuss the strategies; you should know that there are two styles of options based on their expiry date. This is vital information because the option pricing model for both styles of options are different. The two styles of options based on their expiry are:

a) American style options: This style of options can be exercised anytime between the purchase and the expiry date.
b) European style options: This style of options can be exercised only at the expiry date or at rare instances a limited amount of time before the expiry.

The Three Major Models

Now that you are familiar with the two styles of options, let's delve into the three major pricing models.

1. Black Scholes model

The Black-Scholes model is a Nobel prize-winning model and the most popular option pricing model. It was founded in 1973 by two economists: Fischer Black and Myron Scholes. They both received the Nobel prize for their amazing contribution to the field of economics.

The Black-Scholes model was formulated primarily for pricing European options. It is more commonly used because of the assumptions it operates on regarding the underlying stock price and the stock market distribution. The major assumptions the Black-Scholes operate on includes:

a) The implied volatility of the underlying stock is known, continuous, and constant.

b) The continuously compounded returns on the underlying stock are normally distributed and independent over the period of the option.

c) Future dividends are known and fixed.

d) There are zero translation costs and taxes.

e) It is feasible to borrow at the risk-free rate and to short-sell with no cost

However, these assumptions are not fixed. They are often modified and loosened up for special occasions if necessary. The main variables used in the Black-Scholes model calculation includes:

1) Price of the underlying stock

2) The strike price of the option

3) The implied volatility

4) Dividend yield

5) Time until expiration

6) Interest rate

2. Binomial Option pricing

The Binomial options pricing is the simplest method of pricing options. The assumption of this model is that the market is perfectly efficient. Under this assumption, the model can derive the price of the option at any point within a specified time period.

With the binomial model, it is assumed that the price will either go up or down in the allocated time period. Therefore, given the two possible prices of the underlying stock at expiration and the strike price of the option.

The payoff of the option can be calculated under these instances. Then the payoff is discounted to arrive at the price of the option as of today.

3. Monte-Carlo simulation

On the other hand, the Monte-Carlo simulation is one of the most complex option pricing models. Under the Monte-Carlo simulation, the future possible stock prices are simulated based on several factors such as volatility, strike price, market distribution, dividends, and so on.

The simulation is then used to find the option payoff. The option payoff is discounted to arrive at the current option price.

As I said above, option valuations models are sophisticated. They are well beyond the scope of this book and you are more likely to get confused if we go into them. The good news is that your financial adviser can easily make this easier for you. Many exchange trading platforms also possess the tools that can perform these calculations for you.

Now that you have learned what stock options are and how they work. It's time to introduce you to the many ways you can start investing in stock options.

Stock Option Trading

There are basically two ways to trade in stock options; these are over-the-counter(OTC) options and exchange trading.

1. OTC

Over-the-counter trading is a private trade between two willing parties. These options are not listing on the options markets. There is more freedom with OTC trading as the terms can be modified for the benefits of both sides. Generally, the option writer of an OTC is an established economic institution so as to prevent credit debt.

OTC is preferable because it essentially bypasses the market. There is no need for the transactions to be advertised and there are little to no regulatory requirements.

However, for an OTC trade to work, each party must establish a credit line with each other. This is to ensure that both parties will fulfill their obligations.

Counterparties must also conform to their custom agreement, commissions, and settlement procedures.

2. Stock Options Exchange

Even though OTC trading might be preferable to some traders. The easiest and simplest way to trade options is through the standardized options contracts that are listed by various options exchanges (Montreal exchange, Eurex exchange, NYSE Arca, etc).

Exchange-traded options have standardized contracts and are settled with the help of a clearinghouse guaranteed by The Options Clearing Corporation (OCC). These options are standardized. This signifies that any trade carried out on the exchange has a backup guarantee.

Therefore, accurate pricing models are available to everyone. The listing and prices of options can similarly be tracked and looked up easily on these exchanges.

There are a lot of advantages that come with trading on an exchange, that doesn't come with OTC trading. Every exchange publishes a never-ending, live market for the stock options and the options are constantly updated.

This enables independent investors and counterparties to discover opportunities and execute transactions with no delay. The exchange serves as the intermediary to both parties involved in the option transaction.

Fulfillment of the contract is guaranteed by the exchange and there is no need for counterparties to establish a credit line. Both parties trading on an option can remain anonymous while being guaranteed that their contract will be fulfilled.

The exchanges regulate the market by enforcing their strict rules of fairness and transparency. They also maintain the order of the market, especially during rapid and volatile trading conditions. Lastly, the exchanges offer traders alternative to fulfilling their contracts such as "cashless exercises" and "automatic exercise" for call holders.

How Stock Options are Taxed

We'll be closing our discussion by looking at how stock options are taxed. Because even though you don't like it. You will often need to pay taxes after exercising your options.

The good news is that the taxes are not fixed and it's not always. There is a catch—the tax you pay depends on how long you wait between exercising and selling, and the kind of options you dealt in.

Options can be classified into two based on tax treatment.

1) **Incentive stock options (ISO)** - These are rare options usually reserved for top employees and executives. They receive special tax treatments from the federal government.

2) **Non-qualified stock options (NQSO)** - These are the most common options found on exchanges. They receive zero special treatment from the federal government.

ISO is the best type of option you can invest in. They operate under special consideration from the government; you do not pay a tax when you exercise your ISOs. You get to keep all your profit which is otherwise known as the bargain element.

Although, if your bargain element (the total amount you have to gain on exercise) is huge and amounts into several hundred thousands of dollars, it will be submitted to the alternative minimum tax (AMT).

Your bargain element is the difference between the strike price and the underlying market price multiplied by the number of contracts.

If a trader exercised 15 call contracts at an exercise price of $75 and the underlying share sells at $85 on the market. The bargain element will be $15000. The trader stands to make a gain of $10 per share, this multiplied by 15 contracts gives $15000.

Bargain element = (85-75) x(15x100) = $15000. This is not the total profit because the premium and commissions are yet to be subtracted.

Still, you are not entirely free from taxation with your ISOs. When you eventually decide to sell those shares from the ISO options, you will pay a tax on the sale. If you attempted to sell the shares as soon as you exercised them, the total worth of the shares would be treated as regular income and taxed. Mind you, these tax rates can be as high as 40%.

The only way out of this is to hold on to the shares for at least a year and a day after exercise. The tax rate you pay after this waiting period will be at the rate of long-term capital gains. This is considerably lower than regular income tax rates.

Even in spite of this, ISOs are still better compared to the other class of options.

With NQSO, you are not exempt from straightforward taxation. All your NQSO bargain element will be listed as regular income on exercise. Normally, you pay two taxes with every Non-qualified stock option.

When you exercise these options, the company granting you the stocks will list your bargain element as part of your income in your Wage and Tax statement. Therefore, if you made $15000 dollars as a bargain element, you will pay income tax on that $15000 at exercise regardless of whether you sell the shares or not. This tax is known as compensation taxes.

That's not all. When you do decide to sell those shares, you will pay another tax based on his long you have held them. If you sell your stares immediately or within one year of the exercises. The transaction will be reported and taxed as short-term capital gain.

But if you hold on to the stocks for over a year after exercise before selling. The sale falls under long term capital gains. The tax rates on long term capital gains are significantly lower than regular rates.

You must know this because going into options trading requires a lot of patience. In options trading, you save money the more you wait.

Bottom line

So far so good, we have covered everything a beginner needs to know about stock options in this chapter. This chapter is a lot. You are advised to read it slowly, and preferably more than once before taking off to the next chapter; so as to grasp all the basics.

Next chapter, we'll examine the pros and cons of trading stock options from both sides.

Chapter Two
The Good And The Bad

Options as we now know it has been with us for more than 40 years. Exchange-traded options began trading in 1973. However, at that time, many investors have mixed feelings regarding options and other derivatives. They believe options are too complicated and they'll never be able to figure it out in time to profit from it.

The popular belief was that options are incredibly risky investments meant for only the seasoned experts. Truly speaking, the critics of options are not totally wrong, but that doesn't mean they are completely right either.

Stock options, like any other financial investment, is a tool. The right tool will always be invaluable to those who know how to use it. Give a sword to a farmer and its useless. Give that same sword to a soldier and he can win battles with it.

It's the same with options. The good news is that options are finally getting the attention they deserve. These days, there are numerous examples of traders who have benefited from them. These are typically people who only took the time to learn before they started trading. And they were able to benefit from options trading.

However, because there is always a bad side to every story. Many have suffered dearly trading in stock options. This is because they nor their brokers had the proper training.

And, that's the truth of the matter, options can be dangerous. But so is any tool that is ever used wrongly.

In this chapter, you will learn both the advantages and disadvantages of trading stock options. But before you do that, there is an important question that needs to be answered.

Why Use an option at all?

To satisfy the skeptic in you, stock options were invented for two major reasons. Calls were invented as a financial tool that makes a profit on the correct speculations. While Puts were invented as a financial tool that limits losses on a financial asset and doubles as an insurance policy. These are the two major justifications for the existence of options.

1. Speculation

Speculation is a gamble on the future performance of a stock. If a trader thinks a stock price is poised to rise in the near future. Naturally, the next step as an investor is to buy those shares off the market.

However, instead of buying the stock outright; call options offer you a reward for guessing right on the stock movement. With call options, you attain the right to purchase the improved shares at a cheaper rate and all you have to do is pay a little amount.

As a speculator, you are guaranteed to make consid0erable profits on those shares compared to investors who bought the shares immediately. But that's only if you guessed right.

2. Hedging

It's the other way for put options. Puts were designed primarily for shareholders looking for ways to cut their losses. Instead of short-selling the stocks that are about to plummet.

Put options offer investors the ability to profit from the price fall. For investors that guessed right, they get to sell their plummeting stock at a premium price. Therefore, instead of running at a loss, they make a tidy profit. However, that's only if they guessed right.

The Upsides of a Stock options

The points above are the two major reasons why options came into existence. However, the current advantages of using options in the present moment have spiraled beyond these.

Stock options trading is now more preferable and often more profitable to trading directly on the underlying assets for several reasons.

1. Cost-effectiveness

To understand the cost-effectiveness of stock options. Take a look at the Facebook stock price. As of the writing of this book, a single share trades at $216. Let's assume that you forecasted that the stock price will go up later this year due to the coronavirus pandemic.

So, you are interested in 1000 FB shares. This is a sound investment. FB stocks have recorded fantastic growth and are showing no signs of fatigue. However, buying 1000 FB shares will set you back the sum of $216,000. That is not a small amount of money.

On the other hand, if you were to purchase ten $10 calls with a strike price of $216 lasting from October to December. The total cost will only be $20,000(10x 100x$20). This is still a substantial amount of money, but it's insignificant compared to $216,000. Buying the option leaves you with $196,000 that can be used at your discretion, while still offering the same position on the stock.

Obviously, this is an overview of how it works. Stock options are quite not that simple. As an investor, you still have to pick the right call to purchase. You need to do your research. You are an investor, not a gambler.

As a shrewd investor, every call you purchase should be a calculated risk. You have to pick the right call that mimics the underlying stock position properly. But, even with the risk, it's undeniable that options are quite cheaper than stocks.

2. Lesser risk

There are instances where options are riskier than owning equities. Especially, when you are using advanced strategies to trade.

In most instances though, options have a lower risk compared to other equities. The bottom line is that the risk on a particular option depends on how they are used and on what side of the transaction you are.

To an investor holding an option, they are less risky because of two reasons: a) Options are generally cheaper compared to the underlying financial assets, and b) If the option were to expire unexercised. The only money lost is the premium.

Owning stocks is not as safe as owning an Option. Options are the best forms of hedging by far. This is because they are impervious to the surprise catastrophes that sometimes happen in stock trading.

Let me paint a scenario for you. Usually, when an investor buys a stock; a stop-loss order is placed as a form of a hedge. This is placed to protect the investor position.

The order is designed to stop losses when the shares go below a target price specified by the investor. When the stock price goes below the target price, the shares are sold immediately on the market.

Let's assume a particular investor bought two thousand FB stocks four months ago at $208. To cut her losses, she set a stop-loss order of $195 on the stock. Should the price ever fall below $195, all her shares will be sold.

Everything looks safe, right?

Don't jump to such conclusions. The weakness of stop-loss orders lies in its nature. It is an automated tool and it only works when the market is on.

The order works during the day but it can lead to nightmares during the night. Say this coming Saturday morning. The first thing our investor hears on CNN after she woke up is that Mark Zuckerberg is going to have a divorce. And that Instagram's CEO recently made some racist tweets—which has led to the loss of several key investors.

Suddenly, those incredible Facebook stocks deteriorated to a meager $99. But you might be thinking, "Facebook is one of the largest companies on earth, surely they can bounce back." This is probably true. Facebook might eventually recover. But this will probably take several months or years.

But even in spite of the trader's hopes. Since the stop-loss order has been activated, the shares will be sold automatically at $99 when the market opens.

If you are wondering if this happens. It does. A surprise like this happens all the time. In October 2016, Twitter stocks dipped a massive 27%. And this is precisely where options turn out to be the better deal.

If the trader had purchased put options with a strike price of $205, she would be safe from that catastrophic loss. She would be able to sell her shares at a higher rate. This is because, unlike stop-loss orders, options do not shut down when the market closes.

Hence, they are more dependable.

With stocks, your losses can be unlimited. You can lose everything if the parent company files for bankruptcy and the market price of your shares falls to zero.

In the instance in which the price doesn't fall. You only lose the premium you paid to the seller.

3. Higher Potential Returns

With the right forecast, options trading offers a higher percentage return compared to stock trading. Let's say you purchased Apple stocks at $350 six months ago and they rose to $380 in the span of eighteen months. Your profit on each share is $30.

This looks great at a glance. But it is not so if you stopped to consider the cost. You will realize that making a profit of $30 on an investment of $350 in eighteen months is nothing to be proud of. The percentage return is just 8.5%(30/350x100). There are many investment opportunities that yield more in eighteen months.

If you had purchased a $10 Apple call contract with a strike price 350, your profit would be much higher. Your bargain element per call would be $30(380-350). Subtract your option price from the bargain element and you still have a total profit of

$20(30-20) per call. When you calculate the percentage return, it sums to an astounding 200% gain(20/10x100).

4. More Flexibility

As a stock trader, your options are limited to two; you can either stay long on the shares or short them. That's about all you can do. On the other hand, options are very flexible tools. Options offer many ways for investors to turn out their position.

They offer multiples routes to achieving your investment goals. These alternatives are called synthetics. They are considered an advanced option topic and they'll be discussed in the later chapter of this guide.

For instance, shorting a stock is not quite as easy on the stock market. Many brokers charge hefty margins that effectively handicaps investors from shorting their stocks. This can leave you frustrated at the black and white lethargy of stock trading.

Options give you more choices in this regard. In options trading, you have a myriad of choices. You trade not only in stock movement, which can be very stagnant but also in volatility and time value. You can sell options to make a profit on stagnant stocks. You can also buy options to profit from the stocks that are about to have a huge shift.

Shrewd investors combine the purchase and sale of calls and put to profit from any type of price action. Also, as an option holder, you can trade out your position to other traders.

The more in the money an option becomes, the more valuable it becomes to other investors. So no matter the market behavior, there is a strategy that can benefit from it.

5. Profit through Premium sale

The last major advantage of call options is the ability to generate safe income through covered calls. In options trading, you can generate income by switching roles and selling options contracts.

The best way to do this is to own the underlying stocks. Let's say, you have some stocks that have appreciated greatly since you bought them.

You can write a call with a strike price that corresponds to the current market price of the stocks or a higher price and collect a premium. In options trading, this strategy is known as writing a covered call.

If the market price drops below the strike, the option will expire unexercised, and you get to keep the premium and your shares. The premium cushions your own personal loss on the stock market.

However, if the stock price goes up, you sell the shares at the strike price to close the contract. You still get to keep the premium and all the profit you have made on the stocks prior to the sale.

The Downsides of an Option

This discussion is not complete if we don't examine the downside of stock options trading.

Apart from the fact that options are inherently risky investments and a trader can lose all the money invested. There are several other major disadvantages associated with options trading not found in trading other financial assets. Let's take a look at them.

1. Potential Gains Only

Even though it's quite possible to make the right forecasts once you do your background work. The fact remains that options will always be a calculated risk.

In this instance, an option can be likened to playing the lottery. You can figure out the algorithm, but you can still be surprised.

When you buy stocks, you have an actual stake in that stock. You retain the full value of the shares in addition to regular income in the form of dividends. On the other hand, buying an option only affords you a potential long position on the underlying stock.

You don't actually own or earn anything.

In options trading, smart investors use a lot of calculations. Generally, they depend heavily on risk profiles which shows the expected losses and gains based on each strategy. However, no matter how careful or detailed these risk profiles are, they all have the basic flaw of assuming the implied volatility will be constant.

So, at times, it's quite possible for the market to embarrass you. It is absolutely possible for the market to go the way you predicted, and you still fail to make the large profits imagined. The market may end at $1 above the strike price or at the strike price when you expected it to go $5 above.

When you invest in options, you are playing a potential game. You stand to win a little or a lot or everything. If you don't have the stomach for volatile markets and great risk-taking, then options aren't for you.

2. Limited time to exercise

Another downside of stock options is the time factor. Options give you a specified period to exercise your options. It's quite worse with European options that grant you only a couple of hours.

As a shareholder, you can sit on the stock for all eternity as long as it never dips below your stop-loss order. When Facebook went public in 2012, it went out with a market price of $38 per share. If you invested in those stocks eight years ago, each of your shares would be worth $218 right now. This is impressive, that's a staggering percentage increase of 473% in eight years.

If you had invested two hundred thousand dollars in FB shares in 2012, your shares would be worth over a million right now.

Warren Buffet and several other billionaire investors amassed billions by sitting quietly on stocks for decades. As an options investor, this possibility is closed to you. You are expected to make a decision in the time allocated to you. You can't wait forever like Warren buffer. You have days, weeks, or months to make your decision. If you fail to make a decision, the option will expire and you lose 100% of your premium.

Trading out your options is not the best option either because of the time decay associated with options. If you bought a 3-month option at a contract price of $5, and you held it for 2 months. The value is going to drop significantly and you will only be able to trade it for $1-2 or less. This is because it is now a one month option, hence its less valuable.

3. Absurd Requirements

You can decide at any time to purchase one hundred thousand dollars worth of Netflix shares for your newborn baby. You may hope that the shares will rise a hundredfold in 20 years. If this happens, your daughter will have access to millions as an inheritance when she comes of age.

This is the beauty of stock trading. Anyone can trade in them as long as they have the money. You don't need to have a serious financial background. You can either buy those stares yourself or go through a stockbroker, it's your choice. You can even buy shares online these days from within the confinement of your home. That's how easy it is to buy stocks.

But stock options? It's not that easy.

Unless you are entitled to employee stock options, which has its own long list of disadvantages. Before you can start trading listed options, you need to get approval from your broker. You would be asked several questions about your portfolio, investing experience, available financial means, and how far you understand the risk.

After getting that approval, you still don't have full autonomy immediately. Your broker will assign you an Options trading level. This level determines the types of options you can write or purchase and how much you can invest. As you gather experience, your broker will gradually increase your level until you will have access to more dangerous options.

As an industry requirement, every option trader must have a minimum of $2000 in their brokerage account at all times. But on the bright side, this a little price to pay for the opportunity option trading offers.

4. Taxes

Because of the astronomical taxes options are subject too, several investors operate their options strategy from an IRA account or another, similar tax-deferred account.

Apart from ISOs and some special instances, all gains gotten from exercising options are taxed as a short-term capital gain. The rates are the same as your personal income tax rates. This can be painful if you have to exercise a huge amount of options. This is the reason trading from a tax-deferred account is advised.

However, this is not feasible for everyone. The other choice—which is waiting for one year so you can pay long-term income tax isn't so great either.

Anything can happen to stock within the span of one year. You can end up making an additional profit or loss all the profit you gained. But, you can't always count on stocks to stay on your side. Stock can be as volatile as they are sluggish.

5. Commissions

If you think some stockbrokers charge high commissions. Then, I'm happy to inform you that the commission rates for options are higher compared to stocks. Even some options lasting a few weeks have commission rates that are unbelievably high.

Therefore, you are advised to always read all the details of an option contract before you make a purchase. Several brokers will send you newsletter omitting their commission. Only for you to exercise your options and realize that 30% of your earnings will be going to the broker.

Don't be mislead by shady brokers, always inquire about their commission. This way, you will be fully aware of the amount of risk you are undertaking.

6. Reduced earning for shareholders

You must always be on the lookout for companies that offer employee stock options as incentives. Employee stock options are a broad topic and have a chapter dedicated to it later on.

But for now, suffice to say that employee stock options hurt all the shareholders of the company that offers it.

When stock options are exercised, it reduces the total earnings of that company at zero cost to the employees exercising the option. This can lead to poorer performance of the stocks on the market.

And that's not all. It's quite common for companies to purchase stocks off the market for the employees exercising their options. This is done at a loss to the company's total income. That doesn't bode well for the performance of that stock at that time.

7. Unlimited losses for the seller

Lastly, the worst disadvantage of stock options falls on the seller. If the option seller guessed wrong, they can end up losing an astonishing sum of money.

In the instance of a stock doubling in price during the exercise period, the seller can end up with a loss of 200%. Even with a covered call, it's not pleasant selling out shares for a price way below what they are worth.

And as for the put seller, it doesn't matter what price the stocks sell at. The stocks may have a market price of zero, and the seller would be forced to purchase them at the strike price. This is the risk associated with being an option seller.

Bottom line

You have now learned the pros and cons of options trading taking a detailed look at both sides of the trade. Options trading is a wonderful investment opportunity for those with the right knowledge and temperament. Options have a lot to offer if used correctly.

However, they are not without their downsides. But still, those downsides pale in comparison to the upsides if options are employed in the right strategy.

In the later chapters, we'll discuss in detail the various Stock Options strategies. But before that, you will learn the history of stock options in the next chapter.

Chapter Three
Evolution Of Stock Options

The earliest history of stock options can be traced back to Ancient Greece, as far back as the days of Aristotle. Since then, stock options have evolved throughout different eras in history to arrive at the present formal and regularized options we know.

Below, you will learn the notable moments in the evolution of stock options and how they came to be what you are now familiar with.

THE BEGINNING

Isn't it fascinating that options started with a poor man's gamble on the future of olives? I believe it is. The first record of options trade can be traced to Aristotle's book, "Politics". Aristotle made a reference to a man that exploited the market through his invention of " Olive options" as far back as the mid 4th century.

The man's name was Thales of Miletus, he lived in the pre-socratic era, at about 350 B.C. He was a Greek Mathematician, Astronomer, and Philosopher. There are different versions of history as to the reason he created and made use of options. Some said he did it for the riches, some said he did it for the fame.

According to Aristotle, the reason was to prove a point to his fellow Milesians about the benefits of philosophy. However, regardless of what the reason was, the constant factor was that he made a fortune with his invention of olive options

With Thales' knowledge of the weather, he predicted that olives will have a bumper harvest the following year. And at the moment, his prediction was contrary to public opinion.

Being a poor man at the time and reproached for his meaningless philosophy. It was consequently easy for him to exploited the public's perception of him and that of the expected olive harvest.

He created call option contracts for several olive traders and farmers. He then used the little money he had to pay for what we now call premiums, on the bulk of the olive presses that was forthcoming in his surrounding before the harvest season came.

This was possible because nobody would bid against him, everyone thought he was insane to predict a bumper harvest and to even pay them on what was essentially a wager.

Therefore, the value of the contracts was cheap at that time. But as cheap as they were, the contracts gave him the rights to a huge percentage of the olive presses at a fixed price in Miletus and Chios when the harvest season came.

Fortunately, when the harvest season came, it was just as bumper as he predicted. This lead to a surge in demand for olive press and a spike in the prices. He exercised his obligations by purchasing the highly valuable olives at a massive discount.

He then amassed his profit by selling the olives at prices as high as he pleased. He made his fortune, leading to a happy ending and the birth of options.

17th CENTURY: The Tulip Mania

Stock options had another major reference in the Netherlands in the 17th century during what was called "Tulip Bulb Mania." Unlike Thales' story above, this story had a comparative imperfect ending. As mentioned earlier, stock options were still at its infancy and weren't yet the regularized form we have today.

Tulip bulbs, a spring-blooming onion-like plant entered into the European markets very late in the 16th century. It gathered popularity gradually until it collapsed around the late 1630s.

The initial popularity of tulip bulbs started in the early 17th century shortly after a discovery made by Carolus Clusius—a botanist who is a native of southern Netherland. He discovered that tulips could grow in the harsher condition of the Low Landers.

The other reason for its popularity was that Tulips' flower was a unique flower at that time because there were variants of it. Unlike the majority of flowers having a single color or few colors.

The color variants of tulips flower ranged from the single-colored tulips of green, yellow, or white to the multicolored tulips that were more attractive and valuable.

This exotic multicolored variant of the tulips were responsible for its significant use as decoration among the Dutch aristocracy. The increased use of the flowers made tulip bulbs valuable because the flower was obtained by cultivating the bulbs.

Furthermore, its recognition among the Dutch elites enabled its spread into Europe and throughout the world. Thereby contributing significantly to a ravenous demand for tulip bulbs in the 1600s. This leads to the creation of a tunic bulb market by the Dutch.

Initially, during the summer, which is the dormant phase of the plant, tulip bulbs became durable goods that were purchased on spot. After the dormant phase, tulip traders signed legal future agreements(options) that gave them the obligation to buy tulips bulbs and flowers at a discount during spring (the harvest period).

However, due to the increase in the number of concurrent trades of tulip bulbs and flowers going on around the world. Future contracts became much more prominent.

At first, the futures contracts were based more on "the obligations instead of the rights to purchase", in an attempt to minimize the unforeseen loss due to bad harvest or delayed delivery. These earlier options were designed so that the holder can not back out of any agreement.

Between 1610 to 1630s, however, a series of bills were reviewed and passed into law to serve as a moratorium for traders that made future options, it gave them the right to purchase the tulips in the future with minimal risk.

This created a near-perfect market for options trading between the tulip traders; by predicting that the price of the bulb would appreciate a lot in the future, traders entered into a call option to purchase tulips within a specified time in the future.

To purchase this right, the trader would pay a sum of money known as the premium to the bulb seller, which the seller would keep regardless of the bulbs' price in the future.

Through the bills that were passed, the new options replaced the "obligation to purchase" bulbs with the "right to purchase." Thereby reducing the future buyer's risk. In so doing, the bulb option market grew and the value of the tulip bulbs themselves spiked as a result. And so began the tulip bulb bubble.

Tulip traders which included tulip growers and wholesalers would enter into multiple agreements to protect their position due to the instability of the tulip market. Let us not forget that stock options were still evolving at this time, the trades were largely informal and completely unregulated.

As the bulb market spiked in terms of popularity, the value of tulip bulb-option contracts increased as well. This lead to the creation of a secondary market for bulb-option contracts.

In this secondary market, fortunes were made, the general public invested heavily in the market, families sold off their properties, and borrowed money to invest in the tulip bubble market.

Between 1635 to 1637, tulip bulbs options trade quickly spiraled out of control due to the secondary market. Unlike the face-to-face transaction that was done in Thales' era, options trade became a ghost trade.

The Dutch described the market as "Windhandel"("wind trade") because no bulbs were actually changing hands. By this time, the bulbs and the option contracts were changing hands ten times or more a day with increasing prices.

The tulip trades become far too volatile and clearly unsustainable in the long run, but because profits were being made; the trend continued unabated.

At the peak of the bubble, in 1637, tulip bulbs sold for more than 10 times the annual income of a skilled crafts worker. Due to the frenzy and the unreasonably high prices and lack of market regulation. The bubble eventually burst and the supply and price crashed to a near zero.

Families subsequently went bankrupt, millions were lost by the general public and the options traders realized their options were worthless. Even those who technically profited from the market drop failed to do so because there was no regulation and traders failed to honor their deals.

Sellers and buyers began to walk away from their options, nobody wanted to be on the losing end and nobody held anyone responsibly.

Options traders lost their investments and it was so terrible that it led to an economic recession in Netherland. So, as you can see, the ending was definitely not the best of endings.

The 17th century gave options a bad reputation that lasted for centuries.

18th CENTURY

Options relatively went silent in the 18th century after the Tulip Mania. The general public feared stock options and went against it vocally.

Therefore, options trading was limited in Europe. Even though it continued to take place. It went on relatively quietly in some places in England where it was given its own organized market. However, due to the Dutch's experience from the tulip mania era, the number of opposition eventually overwhelmed the quiet option market.

The market for options trading was declared illegal by the British government in 1733. The ban lasted for more than 120 years and it was not lifted until later in the 19th century.

19th CENTURY: Russell Sage And Over The Counter Trade Options

During the 19th and 20th centuries, the evolution of stock options took a leap towards becoming a credible and regulated market. In 1872, stock options were introduced into the New York Stock Exchange by an American financier named Russell Sage.

He is known for the prominent role he played designing options in US trade. Russel is responsible for creating calls and puts as we know them today. He is recognized for creating over the counter(OTC) trade options and organizing the first pricing models based on the duration of the option, the price of the underlying security and interest rates. It was said that he made millions in the process.

Still, these options created by Russell were mostly unregulated, Illiquid, and had very limited participants compared to the tulip bulb era.

Without the regulation, it should be obvious that history was bound to repeat itself. In the market crash of 1884, Russel Sage lost his fortune, and then realizing the inevitable loss behind the options, he stopped trading. However, the role he played in stock options nevertheless remained crucial to its evolution.

In the late 1800s, an upgrade was made on the OTC trade laid down by Russell; the upgrade was the advent of Put and Call Brokers and Dealers around 1895.

These brokers served as middlemen between potential options buyers and sellers. They initially started on the OTC option and later started placing ads on financial journals. They used the adverts to attract buyers and sellers of options contracts with the aim of brokering deals. This created a new market for options formed and regulated by the "Put and Call Brokers and Dealers Association, Inc."

However, even though these trades have more regulated compared to every trade prior; the lack of organized pricing in the options market made most of the options illiquid.

This is because the terms of each option contract such as price and expiration days still had to be determined between the two main parties: the Puts and Calls traders.

Even though the risk was ever-present and there is a remote possibility of the counterparty abandoning the deal and the fact that the majority of the public still did not believe in it.

Stock options markets weathered the storm and it grew steadily in spite of all the shortcomings. So much so that this era of stock options evolution spilled into the 20th century.

20th CENTURY: The Turning Point

The 20th-century is the era the pivoting moment in stock options history. All the major shortcoming accounting for its failure over the centuries were addressed during this time.

In the early years of the century, specifically around 1920; Puts and Calls broker market created an avenue for fraudulent activities that started back in the late 1800s through bucket shops.

Bucket shops can be defined "as a brokerage firm that engages in unethical business practices." In simpler terms, Bucket shops deal in fraudulent investments. And these scams were simpler to execute then because the internet was non-existent.

It was tough to verify the legitimacy of any underlying commodities an option is traded on. Therefore, these fraudsters would falsify an increased demand for a worthless stock and persuade new investors to invest in it. If you have watched the movie: The wolf of wall street. Then you can understand this.

The aim of these fraudsters is to make away with the investor's money and premiums. So in the early 1900s, these rampant scams in addition to tulip bubble history gave new investors a dilemma over stock options.

However, in the united states, as an urgent response to the Great depression of 1929. Congress hoped to rescue financial markets by creating "The Securities and Exchange Commission (SEC)." This was to serve as a U.S. government oversight agency.

The SEC's mission was to ensure that companies, options brokers and dealers, and exchanges made truthful statements about their businesses, and also treated new investors in an honest and fair manner.

This mandate was established under the "U.S. Securities Act of 1933" and the "Securities and Exchange Act of 1934." But, even though SEC brought some potential stability into OTC options trades, the complexities involved and fluctuating prices made it problematic for investors to accept options as a viable tradable instrument.

In 1935, the turning point came when SEC granted the "Chicago Board of Trade (CBOT)" the license to register as a national securities exchange with no expiration. This decision turned out to be a great boon for stock options even though it took CBOT more than 30 years to act on it.

At the time CBOT was granted the license by SEC, CBOT was an established 120 years old company. They specialized in helping farmers and commodity consumers manage risks by removing price uncertainty from agricultural products such as wheat, corn, and animal products.

However, during the 1960s, the agricultural commodity market plateaued. The CBOT had no option but to start looking for a new line of opportunity. The steady growth of the Stock options trade hinted at was a promising market that would thrive if provided stability.

So, the CBOT came up with a pilot study to create a marketplace for regularized options called Exchange-traded options. The pilot study was approved by the SEC in 1971. The pilot study set up rules to standardize contract duration, strike price, and expiration dates.

They also established a centralized options clearinghouse called Options Clearing Corporation (OCC) through which all options traded through CBOT will be cleared. This ensured that every obligation pertaining to an option contract will be fulfilled in a timely and reliable manner.

By 1973, the pilot study proved to be a rousing success. The CBOT was trading about 6 times the old options trading rate. This lead to the creation of the Chicago Board Options Exchange (CBOE). The CBOE took over from the pilot study and became the first standardized stock options exchange in the world.

By June 1974, the CBOE averages a daily tally of over 20,000 options contracts. However, this success isn't just due to the regularized market. It can be attributed to the works of Fisher Black and Myron Scholes.

They both created a mathematical formula known as the Black Scholes Pricing Model. The formula is used to calculate the price of an option using specified variables. The application of the formula by CBOE lead to the credible growth of the options market in its first year alone.

This formula combined with the regulations of the CBOE brought along the long-awaited stability and security that was needed in stock options. After 1974, investors far and wide started accepting options trading as a viable tradable instrument.

From that point onward, things only got better for stock options. In 1975, bigger investors came into the market. The Philadelphia Stock Exchange and American Stock Exchange opened their own option trading floors. Thus, boosting competition and bringing options to a wider marketplace.

The birth of the internet in the late 20th century led to another significant boost in options markets. Option markets became easily accessible to the general public. Millions of trade were made in a day. For instance, In 2008, the OCC had a record of 30,006,663 option contracts traded in a single day.

THE FUTURE OF STOCK OPTIONS

Gone were the days when stock option transaction was cumbersome, had no security, and no continuous market. The Internet has made it very easy for everyone to trade in options; with so many trading platforms online that are easily accessible with good liquidity rates.

With more regularity, more option pricing models, and faster internet speeds. Options trading can only get better. Looking back to the era of Thales from our present age. The growth is already astounding. There are millions of options contracts being executed on the internet as you are reading this, a number that is increasing every day.

And, with the invention of the American stock option, traders don't have to wait till the expiry date to exercise their options. Several option trading platforms already offer advanced tools that make it possible for traders to make profits through split-second decisions.

There is now access to advanced forecasting and researching tools, market and data charts, and real-time monitoring of the underlying stock. All of which can be accessed through a mobile phone and computer anywhere in the world.

Traders need not wait months and weeks anymore if they don't want to. In the future, these platforms will only get advanced and faster.

New time-dependent strategies not currently feasible will be formulated and deployed. Many old strategies and regulations will be abandoned for better ones. In the future, only those ready to lean into these new technologies will be able to maximize their profits in options trading.

CHAPTER FOUR
Employee Stock Options

Employees stock options (ESO) have been available for decades. The issue in them in the past was that most companies shun them for cash incentives. However, the reverse is now true.

Employee stock options have experienced staggering growth in the past decade. They have come to dominate the pay—and the wealth of major executive in the united states. Altogether, the total sum of unexercised options held by US executives every year is in the sum of billions.

In 1998, Michael Eisner attained over half a billion dollars by exercising his 22 million options. In 2019, both Intel's CEO Craig Barrett and Jack Welch had over three hundred thousand dollars in unexercised options.

It's not an exaggeration to state that the outbreak of employee stock options has changed the face of corporate business worldwide. ESO now offer better prospects to top talents, executives, investors, and entrepreneurs than cash incentive ever could. They also seem to offer little in terms of risk, since the employees pay no premium.

Naturally, there are a lot of critics on ESOs. Critics believe ESOs have poorly understood long-term consequences. They question whether companies really the implication of what they are doing. The critics believe that options motivate top executives to chase short term goals, which could be to the detriment of the company in the long run.

It's a highly controversial topic with vocal supporters on both sides.

However, to a fresh talented employee like you, ESOs can trigger several mixed feelings. On one side, they look like the perfect incentive, and at the same time; they look risky because options can become worthless if the company falters.

It is because of this reason that we have to consider the question: Why are companies even offering ESOs?

Why Companies use ESO

Because there will always be that worldwide competition for top talent and capable officials. Companies resort to various methods to compensate and retain loyal employees that support the company's vision. ESO is just one of these methods.

ESOs gives employees a reason to stay, but not just that. It boosts the collective motivation and job satisfaction of employees.

Employees having ESOs have something to gain if the company grows and succeeds. In a way, the lucky employees granted stock options start seeing things differently.

They get a boost in productivity because they don't just work for salary anymore—they get to share in the company's success through stock holding. If the company grows, they grow; if it falls, they plummet with it.

ESOs provide a physical representation of just how much the company value the employee. It is designed to be a win-win strategy. Companies get ultra-motivated employees and the employees stand to make fortunes from the parent company's success.

It's even better for startup companies. Usually, startups don't tend to have a lot in terms of income. They are still in the process of building something. Yet, to succeed they need top talent they can't afford to pay.

So, in order to offset the below-average salary paid to the workers. Startups offer a lot of stock options to their workers. With this, they get incredible talent working for an abysmally low wage—but with the hope of landing an enormous payday later on.

Understanding Employee Stock Options

Employee Stock Options are very similar to Call Options. You already understand what those are and how they work. Nonetheless, ESOs differ from normal exchange trade calls by operating under several specific conditions. If you are wondering why the conditions?

The restrictions are placed there for the benefit of the company. Nobody in their right minds would grant free options to employees who could abscond with them.

We'll discuss these conditions because you should know them. In the instance, you are offered ESOs in the future. You would be versed in how they work and in knowing what offer to accept (and reject).

That said, the first thing to know is ESOs are not traded on exchanges. ESOs are granted by the grantor (the parent company) to the grantee(the employee).

The grantee has to work for the company in order to have and retail access to the ESO contract. Every ESO grant has a grant date, followed by a waiting period and then a vesting schedule during which employees can exercise their options. There are still some other restrictions apart from this. All of which you will learn as you go through this chapter.

Grant date

The grant date is the date the employee is issued the Option. But unlike an exchange-traded option, these options can't be exercised immediately; even though the grant date is the moment the time starts counting.

At the time of the grant, you only have the option. Not the right to purchase the stocks.

Strike Price

The method by which ESOs arrive at the strike price is quite simple. They are so unlike listed options that often have varying strike prices. Listed options can either be "in-the-money" or "out-of-the-money" and it reflects on the price of the premium.

Contrarily, ESOs are usually "at the money" options because they are issued at the current market price on the day of the grant. This special strike price is popularly known as the "grant price."

Therefore, most ESOs have an intrinsic value of zero. All you have with them is the time value, which is considerably high. Since its fairly common to have ESOs lasting five to ten years.

However, on rare occasions, you can have the strike price discounted to a price lower than the market price on the day of the issue. But this is usually available only to top executives as a form of extra compensation.

Waiting Period

The waiting period starts immediately after the date of the grant, and in most instances, it lasts less than 30% of the option duration. If you were granted an ESO of ten thousand Google's stocks lasting 5 years. Your waiting period, which some investors calls "the cliff period" is the time you have to wait before you can exercise those shares.

Why the cliff period?

It's simple. The company wants you to stay and do your best to make sure it succeeds. If you are granted the right to those shares immediately, you can simply leave the company to work elsewhere.

The cliff period is the time you can actually make a difference for the company. If an employee departs from the company during the cliff period, he/she loses all access to the option.

Vesting schedule

The waiting doesn't end after the cliff period, however. After the cliff period comes the vesting schedule; which is the timetable under which employees gain full control of their granted options.

Continuing our discussion with the Google options above. Over the remaining four years of the option, google may grant you a vesting schedule of 25% per year.

This means you will only be able to exercise 2500(25% of 10000 shares) shares each year until the end of the vesting schedule.

However, this is not a rule of the book.

Vesting schedules vary widely across the industry. Some companies grant options that vest all at once following the cliff period. While in most cases, companies offer a gradual vesting schedule to their employees.

It's all about keeping these employees if you really think about it. ESOs have tremendous advantages in the form of their extended time-value and the fact that the grant price doesn't change. It wouldn't matter if the market price of the stock rises to $248 five years after the grant date. If the grant price was a low $36, the employee will exercise those shares at $36.

If you are wondering if this is possible, this is exactly what happened with Zoom's stocks. They went from $36 at IPO to $248 within 24 months.

Companies offer these autonomous opportunities for fortunes, but they don't want to run at a loss. If an employee can simply leave the company and still retain access to those opportunities; the company would run at a loss.

Therefore, if an employee leaves before the vesting period is over. That employee retains only the rights to the vested options. Let's say, Sandra, a top executive worked for 6 years with Amazon and has 50% of her options vested.

If after 6 years, she leaves Amazon for Alibaba for higher pay, she'll still be able to exercise those shares at any time of your choosing before the expiry date. However, she will lose access to the remaining 50% stock forever.

Expiry date

The expiry date is the date the option expires. Often times, the vesting schedules end before the expiry date. It's possible to have an option lasting eight years with a vesting schedule of five years. If the employee fails to exercise the options throughout the vesting period, the employee still has two years left to make the decision.

Contract Restrictions

The existence of a vesting period gives rise to certain control issues. At times, the requirements for the vesting goes beyond waiting. Companies may demand that the employee meet certain performance or sales targets.

This is usually spelled out in the ESO contract; which is why it's a must every employee read them. Failure to do this often leads to distasteful situations when the unaware employee discovers the restrictions.

Another restriction not attending listed options is the lack of freedom. You can sell the shares you got from a list option anytime you want. You can't always do that with employee stock options.

Often times, the company places certain restrictions forbidding you from selling the acquired shares immediately. This can leave you in an uncomfortable situation. Because you are left with stocks that can depreciate in value.

What you can do with your ESOs

Even with subpar operating conditions, employee stock options are still options. After the vesting period, the available choices are basically the same with exchange-traded options. Unless you have restrictions stopping you from selling your exercised shares—you have 3 choices available to you.

1. Exercise and sell immediately

This is the straightforward choice, you purchase the discounted shares assigned to you. Then, you sell those stocks immediately to make your profit if you can.

2. Sell later

The second possibility is to sit on those shares you exercised. There are several reasons why choosing this is preferable. The first is that there is always the likelihood that the stock price will rise.

The second reason is that unless you are granted incentive stock options, you stand to lose a huge chunk of your profit to short-term income taxes. So keeping those shares for at least a year and a day lowers the taxes you pay when you sell.

3. Sell and keep

The alternative to both choices above combines the best of both worlds. After exercising your options, you can sell some of your shares to cover the cost of purchase and keep the rest. This can be done if you want to make an instant profit, but you are not ready to lose most of it to taxes.

Drawbacks of Exchange-traded options

There is no doubt that Employee Stock Options is one of the best forms of employee compensation. There are several examples of employees making a fortune on ESOs. However, they have some certain drawbacks associated with them that should be considered.

Several of these drawbacks are due to the nature of ESOs. A lot of the freedom associated with exchange-traded options is lost with them.

Even though they may make you a millionaire, it's paramount that you know why they can't replace cash incentives. Here are the drawbacks in detail:

1. Lack of standardization

Two major flaws of ESOs are the fact that their values are hard to calculate and that they are not standardized options. They are typically issued at the money, giving them zero intrinsic value.

On the other hand, listed options have varying prices, depending on the input variables and factors such as the underlying market price and performance.

Therefore, employees holding ESOs are left with options of unknown worth. This is further complicated by the lack of standardization. All listed options have regularized terms regarding the number of shares, strike price, expiration date, and so on.

This standardization makes it's easy to trade out any optionable stock across various exchanges. But with ESOs, your right to exercised those shares is not standardized. Your rights are limited to the company you work for.

2. Lack of automaticity

With listed options, you don't have to always be on the lookout. There are automatic orders that exercise your options for you at expiry as long as they are in the money.

You can of course contact your broker on this to roll back the exercise and allow the option to expire. But that automaticity will always be there with exchange options.

Employee's stock options don't have this. If you don't personally exercise the options, they all expire worthless even if they are in the money.

3. Can't be sold

There is no bigger drawback than this fact right here. According to Investopedia, nearly 60% of stock options are traded out by options holders. Many traders sell off their options, albeit at a lower price when they realize their gamble isn't going to play out. It's the same for options writers too. Many choose to buy back their options, instead of being subject to the disastrous loss that will be incurred during exercise.

As an ESO holder, you can never sell your options. The options may have an exercise period of 10 years and have a potential worth of $100 per contract, but all that doesn't matter. Since you can never sell them.

4. Not guaranteed

The final drawback with Employee Stock Options is the lack of guarantee. The Option clearing corporations serve as clearinghouses for all options contracts and guarantees the compliance of the sellers.

Hence, anyone trading listed options is assured that the counterparty will deliver on their promise.

It's not so with ESOs, the company is the sole guarantor of the options. While this works out fine in most cases. The opposite happens enough to warrant your attention.

You have to be extremely cautious about the financial situation of the company. If the company goes bankrupt or gets acquired by a larger conglomerate, you will be left with valueless stocks or worse still, worthless acquired stocks.

ESO vs other compensations

Having taken a look at the drawbacks of employee options, it is only normal to examine other forms of employee compensation. Being aware of other forms of compensation is invaluable. Not all employee stock options are incredible.

Many can be meaningless promises not worth your time and attention. It's always better to reject useless ESOs if you can get another kind of compensation. Here are examples of other incentives you can consider.

1. Restricted Stock Units (RSUs)

These are a form of stock-based compensation. These are contracts that grant free stocks to an employee.

Similar to Employee Stock Options, they have a vesting period. Before this vesting period, the RSUs have no value. They remain as promises. The employee receives no dividends nor do they attain any rights.

After the vesting period or after achieving the qualifying goals set by the company; the RSU holder receives the allotted shares. Some companies accumulate and pay out the accumulated dividends after the vesting period. Some use the accumulated funds to cover taxes.

RSUs can be preferred to ESOs because they have actual value after vesting. The employee receives real company stock that they can sell immediately or keep for later.

It is also possible for the shares to be sold immediately by the company. In which case the employee receives only cash—but this is not common.

However, even taking the fact that there is the possibility that the shares may plummet during the vesting period and become worthless. RSUs are still preferable because it is free stock.

The employee doesn't get to pay a dime. And there is always a chance the stocks will rise or stagnates. Either way, it has real financial value.

However, unlike some options that have special tax considerations. RSUs are taxed on the market value of the shares at the time of vesting. If the shares are sold immediately, the same is taxed at the ordinary income rate, which can be quite high.

2. Phantom Stocks

Phantom stocks are the compensation plan that gives some special employees the benefits of owning company stocks without buying any shares. This is also known as "shadow stock" or "synthetic equities."

This form of compensation is rarer than stock options. They are reserved for the upper management and for the few outstanding executives who achieved a spectacular goal.

The way it works is that rather than getting real company stocks, the employee gets a mimic stock. But even though the stock is clearly fake—it follows the price movement of the company's real stock, thus paying out dividends.

The phantom stock itself has no value and can not be sold on the market. Although, after a specified period of time, the cash value of the shadow stocks can be paid to the phantom stock owner. The earnings from phantom stocks are always taxed as ordinary income.

3. Stock Appreciation Rights (SARs)

This is a similar program to Phantom stocks. However, rather than earning dividends, the employees get paid an amount equal to the company's stock appreciation over a period of time.

They tend to have a vesting period similar to stock options. They tend to benefit employees willing to stick around hoping that the stock prices rise. The increase in the value of the assigned stocks can be paid either as cash or as stocks. The employee retains no rights to the assigned stocks.

4. Employee stock purchase plan

These are more straightforward than all the alternatives above. With these plans, employees attain the right to purchase company stocks at a discount in the future. But, rather than using strike prices as stock options do, these plans make use of percentages to offer the discount.

4. Cash incentive

As always, the best incentive is a cash incentive. There are no requirements or restrictions or potentiality associated with cash incentives. The employees simply get a paycheck and a fuller bank account.

How to deal ESOs

If you are ever lucky enough to be granted ESOs. The right step to take is to not accept it immediately. Here are two vital steps you should take.

1. Read the contract extra carefully

There is no way to stress this fact enough. Before you accept any ESO contract, you should have a perfect understanding of everything contained in the contract.

Be sure you are aware of all that is required of you, the type of option, and the potential tax treatment. Having to wait an extra year after waiting for five years to exercise your options is not easy or pleasurable.

ESOs can be a burden if they don't have special tax treatment or if they have certain dubious requirements. You may end up doing a lot of work and waiting a lot of time—only to have nothing to show for it.

You are advised to review the contract with your financial advisor before making a decision.

2. Fit the option into your investment plan, not the other way round.

A lot of employees make the mistake of changing their investments plan in order to fit their ESO contracts. This can be a costly and irredeemable mistake. It should be the other way round.

You have to consider how the option and the underlying shares fit into your broader financial goals. Do you even want to own large stocks in the company? Will the exercised shares put you in a too-tight position?

Remember that ESOs often come with restrictions that forbid you from selling the shares immediately. This is not a good thing in stock trading. Having a concentrated stock is dangerous, and it's worse when it's your employer's stocks.

If the company experiences any financial hurdles and the stock falls. You can end up losing a substantial part of your investment and your job.

Please don't be in a hurry to accept the contract. Although the options may offer remarkable opportunities. There is no guarantee that they'll come through. It is wise to make them part of your investment strategy. It's unwise to make them your investment strategy.

Have that big investment goal that can still succeed without your ESO granted shares. This way, if the company falters, you will still have other backup investments elsewhere.

ESO hedging strategies

Now, after accepting that ESO contract that convinces you. The next step isn't to keep working and hoping for the best. You are taking on a gamble accepting the contract. And there are actually some strategies you can employ to mitigate the risk associated with the options. We'll be considering two of these.

1. Write calls

Writing calls for stocks you don't own is one of the riskiest choices available to you in the world of investment. You are advised not to ever do this. The good news is that if you write calls for your ESOs stocks, they'll be covered.

Let's assume that three years ago, you were offered 10 Employee Option contracts by your company with a grant price of $50. Now the current market price of the stocks is $80 and you still have 3 years before the expiry of the option.

To hedge your earnings, you can write a call of $90 for the vested options. These calls can go as high as $30 per call because of the extended time value.

If you do this, you can receive as much as $30,000 in premium for the calls. This call is safe because you can still buy the stocks at any time at a discount price of $50.

Therefore, if the stock trades below the strike price over the next three years, you can pocket the premium and still be able to exercise your options.

However, if your options are called away, you get to receive $90 for every share you purchased at $50 and you still have the premium on top of that.

This is where the extended time value of Employee Options comes into play. And, if you have more than a year left to exercise your options, you can always write more than one call. You can write a call that last six month, followed by one that lasts a year and so on.

2. Buy Puts

The other alternative is to buy puts. If you are not quite the optimist regarding the company's future, you can purchase annual puts for your options.

With the current stock price being at $80, you can buy 10 at-the-money put contracts of $10 each. This will cost you about $10000 in premium charges.

If you guessed right and the stock trades below $70, you can still recoup the cost of the premium by exercising those options.

However, if the stocks perform well above the $80 at or before expiry. You lose the premium. The reason why this hedging strategy is preferable to writing calls is that you are not obligated to sell your shares. You can simply make the decision most preferable to you.

Bottom line

Employee Stock Option is one of the ways companies compensate their best employees and executives. It is comparable to regular call options; in that, they give employees the right to buy shares at a discounted price in the near future.

Even though they are far from being the best forms of compensation. They have a long list of reasons they should be considered such as their zero cost and the long expiry date. However, the fact that they are not regularized options also gives them their fair share of disadvantages. This makes them inappropriate for everyone.

And that's why it's paramount that ESOs contracts are well understood before they are accepted. Next chapter, we'll take a brief look at the common mistakes traders make dealing with listing options and how you can get up to speed.

Chapter Five
Getting Up To Speed

In line with our discussion so far. You would agree that Options trading is definitely more complicated than stock trading. The amount of choice and flexibility that comes with options trading comes at the expense of simplicity. Hence, there is an increased risk of making mistakes.

Therefore, as a beginner hoping to make a profit in option trading, there are certain things you are required to know. Having this knowledge will get you up to speed and help you avoid some costly mistakes. That said, the first thing you have to know about options trading is that...

You are on your own

Owning stocks can be very simple—you simply shop through a licensed broker that trades on your behalf. If you are in it for the long term, you need not be bordered by the gibberish of stock trading, the red and green flashes of Nasdaq on your TV, or the bizarre stock trading data CNBC spews daily.

You can do well by just understanding the basics of stock trading, setting your stop-loss orders, and keep on raking in your dividends. Your broker can manage your stocks for decades and all you have to do is pay their fair commissions.

But, if you are an option holder? It's not so easy.

Stock option traders are expected to be self-directed investors. Even though you still have to trade options through a broker. The brokers don't manage your options trading portfolio for you. Thus, as an options trader, you have complete control over your transactions and trading decisions.

Even taking into account the massive development in options trading—the level of automation and all. You are still in full control of using these automated processes. Plainly speaking, you are all on your own. You are one hundred percent responsible for your decisions in the options trading market.

Understanding the stock option quotes

As explained earlier, you can either trade in OTC options or exchange-listed Options. Option exchanges like the NYSE list several million stock options daily in the form of quotes.

To choose the right options, it's paramount that you understand all the details of the stock option. This is where beginners often run into problems because stock options quotes look too simple.

However, they contain all the important data you require to make your decision—such as cost, type of option, and expiry date.

Here's what a quote looks like and how to understand it.

> **Microsoft October 30, 2020 205 Call at $5**
>
> Red = *Underlying Stock*
> Yellow = *Date of expiration*
> Green = *Strike price*
> Blue = *Type of option*
> White = *Premium*

Costly Mistakes to watch out for

The two terms that lead to the quick demise of options traders are Greed and Fear. As Mahatma Gandhi once proclaimed "Earth provides enough to satisfy every man's needs, but not every man's greed."

Every day, tons of reasonable options are listed. It takes a logical and forward-thinking mind to leverage these options. Similarly, a lot of awful options are listed daily. But, because of greed and the fear of losing out. Beginners, more often than not, end up with these poor options.

Hence, as a beginner, there are endless possibilities of walking into a pitfall that can break your morale. This doesn't have to be so. Even though options will always be risky endeavors, there are some silly mistakes that can be avoided to tip the odds in your favor. Let's go over them.

Mistake 1: Getting lured by inexpensive options

As of this writing, Disney Inc. stocks trade for $115 per share. If I want three thousand of those shares, it'll set me back $339,000. On the other hand, I can buy a three-month contract of $125 Disney Inc. calls for as low as $1. Buying 30 contracts will cost me just $3,000.

This looks like a good deal at first glance. *If I'm lucky and Disney trades above $125 at or before expiry, I can make a massive profit, right?*

No.

This is a poor strategy because stocks rarely move that fast. In the real world, it's far more likely that the there month goes by and Disney stocks never rise that high. In which case I'll lose the entire premium.

This is the most common mistake beginners make when they start trading options. They often get scared by the prices of in-the-money options and believe they can bag a huge gain with cheap options.

More often, though, they lose all their investment. Since stocks rarely experience rapid upward surges, which is the reason out-of-the-money options are perpetually dirt cheap.

Truly speaking, there is nothing wrong in forecasting and buying out-of-the-money options with money you can lose. It's simply unwise to make your bet on them. Unless you have some background strategy that they fit into or you have the money you can as well spend on sports betting. Please stay away from cheap options.

Mistake 2: Over-investing

It takes some doing to get used to options trading after coming straight from stock trading. Stocks are expensive commodities, while, options being derivatives are quite cheap.

Presently, buying two thousand Netflix shares will set you back an amount close to a million dollars. Meanwhile, buying 20 2-month in the money calls or puts might cost you less than ten thousand dollars.

The second pitfall beginners often fall into is investing too much too fast. This decision is driven both by greed and fear. The opportunity to make so much profit on so many stocks at a fraction of the cost is a temptation too much for some.

But, don't be deceived by the cheap prices of options. Don't let your emotions drive your decisions. Remember that options are derivatives. Even the best option strategy can go wrong.

The best recommendation is to limit your losses to 1-7% of your portfolio per trade. Don't ever go beyond 10%. Don't be too greedy. This way, if a trade goes wrong, you have a backup to start again on other trades.

Mistake 3: Not doing enough analysis

Options trading is not the same as gambling. You should never resort to guessing in trading options because every decision should be based on rational thinking. Therefore, one of the hallmarks of a successful trader is having a frame of reference for their options trade.

The commonest building block of this frame of reference is the ability to analyze options. There are two main analysis styles you need to familiarize yourself with: Fundamental and Technical.

Fundamental analysis means reviewing the underlying company's performance in the past, financial statements, and current business trends so as to have an accurate view of the company's worth.

Technical analysis includes reviewing the volume and price of the company's stock while looking out for areas of resistance, price variation, and supports so as to be able to pinpoint opportunities.

Both analyses combined enable you in making a better forecast. Even though according to the efficient market hypothesis, it's virtually impossible to make an accurate prediction on the market direction. With the right analysis. You'll be able to know when you are taking a gamble apart from when you are taking a calculated risk.

In options trading, there is no room for guesswork. As you review your options strategy, it's paramount you don't follow your gut feeling. Take your time to do the required research and analysis.

Mistake 4: Ignoring the implied volatility

High implied volatility points to a bearish market for the underlying stocks. This means investors are losing confidence and pulling back. Low implied volatility is the exact opposite of this—in which case investors are gaining confidence.

The higher the volatility, the more expensive the option. You should know volatility is never based on guesswork. It's the measure of how the market expects the stocks to behave and several other variables. Option sellers always calculate their option price using the implied volatility.

It's vital you take this into account in your frame of reference. It'll enable you in choosing options with the right prices matching your strategy.

The problem with Beginner is that they don't do this. They often make the mistake of ignoring this simple variable and unknowingly go for cheaper options with low volatility. The good news is that volatility data are always easily accessible. You should study them carefully before making your decisions.

Mistake 5: Not managing time correctly

As an options trader, time is your most valuable resource. The time you have to exercise any of your options is limited. The first pitfall regarding time has already been covered. Buying a short-term option is not the best strategy. The more time you have to exercise your options, the better.

But, this isn't always the rule.

The second pitfall is mismanaging the time you have. There are a lot of reasonable short-term options. The attribute that determines if anyone profit from them is the ability to manage time.

Imagine you have five $80 call contracts on a stock that just went up to $89. The calls have an expiry period of 12 weeks, you have held them for 9 weeks and they cost you $5 each. Taking away the commission and taxes, you stand to make a profit of $2,000 if you exercise immediately. This is not bad considering your investment was $2500.

However, the problem is that you still have 3 weeks on the contract. You ask yourself: Is this the right time to exercise?

The answer to this is **YES**.

If you are thinking that it is still possible that the stocks go up. That is your greed talking. Thinking solely on the expiry date is not a good habit. It's vital that you understand your position at all times.

In the situation above, you stand to make a significant profit while minimizing your losses. It's, of course, possible that you may make more profit if the market moves up. But it's similarly possible that you lose everything if the market goes against you in the span of 3 weeks.

You should always consider the risk/reward of your indecision when trading options. Is it worth waiting if you stand to lose the current advantage? Do you have more to lose or to gain?

The answer to this is always vital in options trading. It's not a must to wait till the expiry, it's prudent to exercise as long as you have a reasonable profit to make.

Mistake 6: Lacking a trading goal and exit plan

To be a successful trader, regardless of the type of trade, it's vital that you have a trading and exit plan. You have limited time and choices to make. And I mentioned earlier—fear and greed can lead to many unwise decisions.

Hence, the necessity of a trading plan.

Yes, your goal is to make money, but you have to be crystal clear about how to do that and how much you want to make. There are many questions that need answering:

- Are you aiming to keep the premium?

- What profit margin are you aiming for?
- How soon will you trade out if the price goes the wrong way?

You need to answer all these questions. To succeed, your plan needs to cover the following:

- How to leverage opportunities in the market.
- Knowing how much you are willing to risk.
- When to trade.
- What profit is enough.
- How to reduce risk.

Also, in the instance the trade doesn't go your way, you should have an exit plan ready to go. You should know when to pull out of a trade. For instance, if a trade isn't going your way, you can have a plan to trade out or call back the option.

Having a plan removes the bias of emotion from your trading. It also helps you sleep better at night. Planning makes trading easier. It's easier to learn from your mistake when you have a plan.

You can keep repeating what works and trying out new strategies. Without a plan, however, all your trades would be guesswork.

I know there is the argument that you may be leaving money on the table with exit strategies. However, it's vital to remember that the goal of options trading is not reaping sudden huge gains, but making consistent gains over time.

Mistake 7: Trying to make up for past losses

Another common mistake beginners make is doubling down on current trades because of past losses. A lot of times, traders swear not to repeat a certain mistake they made in the past.

But then they get into a trade and rather than buying the usual reasonable amount of options, they invest more in riskier options hoping to recoup some past losses.

But emotions have no place in a trade.

Things might be going your way now, but it wouldn't always be that way. You might be tempted into buying more options when the market is favorable to you. Be very careful and don't be tempted by greed.

This is because luck also goes the other way. A trade can turn sour any moment and leave you with significant losses. Don't fail to pull out of bad trades because you want extraordinary profits.

If your target profit is reached, take it and don't wait for a second longer. Also, if the market is going against you and you have the opportunity to buy back your position at a marginal loss, do it and reevaluate your strategy. Don't hope to regain past losses.

Mistake 8: Waiting too long to buy back your options

There is no mistake worse than this. As an option seller, you carry most of the risk and your profit is limited to the premium.

A lot of newbie sellers fail to buy back the short options earlier. You should remember that options have a decaying time value. The close it gets to expiry, the lesser it's worth.

When a trade is going your way, it's easy to smile and hope it continues that way but that's not what always happens. Whenever you have the chance to buy back your position close to expiry, it is important you do it.

Assuming you sold out 3 months out of the money options at $2 and it's worth after 2 months is $0.5. It's only safe to buy if back at that time. 40 cents are not worth the risk of waiting a month. If you wait and the market goes the wrong way, you can end up losing far more than you bargained for.

Mistake 9: Trading Illiquid Options

It's worth mentioning that you should only trade in liquid options. This helps because when you want to cut your losses

It's easier to do that with liquid options while it's more expensive to buy out of illiquid options.

Liquidity means there is a high volume of active traders on the options at all times. Stocks are generally more liquid than options because options are numerous compared to options. A single stock may have thousands of options on it at any time.

The things you should look out for to see if an option is liquid includes:

1. **How in the money it is:** Options are generally more liquid the more in-the-money they are.
2. **The number of open contracts:** The more volume traded per day, the better. Any option you trade in should have at least a number of open contracts fifty times the amount you want to purchase. This makes getting out easier.

Mistake 10: Not calculating dividends

Soon, you will come across some options that seem to have all the right variables and yet appear inexpensive. The problem with these options will often be glaring when you consider the dividends.

When you calculate the dividends some stocks payout, they may end up equaling or surpassing what you have to gain if you bought the option. If you come across these options, it's preferable to buy the stocks instead.

Why?

Options are not guaranteed. The market can always go against your best bet. If dividends surpass the reasonable gains you stand to make. There is no point in investing in the options. So always take dividends into account when making your strategy.

How to choose an option trading platform

Now that you have learned how to avoid the common mistakes in option training. You should know that learning the common mistake will only get you half the way. The other decision that will determine your success is the platform you choose.

The importance of the right broker and trading platform can not be stressed enough. Options trading can be complicated with the wrong broker. However, with the increased competition, a lot of brokers now offer astounding services that make your life easier.

So, here are four major traits you should look for before choosing a broker.

1. Customer service

Always put your broker's customer service to the test. How reliable are they? Are they available 24/7 or on weekdays? What communication method do they prefer? How often do they respond?

Reach out to them and test all these parameters out before signing on.

2. Free education

Options trading is an evolving market, even experts get surprised so they learn new things every day. Being a beginner, it's a must that your broker offers a lot of free training resources.

Before you start trading, it's only logical to learn a lot through your broker's free education. This can be in many forms: online courses and eBooks, webinars, face-to-face, and one-on-one training and on phone, and so on.

Another tool you should be on the lookout for is simulations. Some brokers offer a simulated version of their options trading platform. Use this to test-drive the platform and to familiarize yourself with the platform before registering.

3. Consider the versatility of the platform

Researching and performing an unending analysis of data is the summary of the life of an options trader. You need to make sure your broker offers you enough tools to do this efficiently.

Some of the basic tools to look out for includes:

- Calculators for maximum upsides and downsides of options
- Screening tools
- Updated quotes feed
- A chart program for picking entry and exit points

As you transform into an expert trader, you'll need advanced tools to support your complex strategies. Advanced tools offer better screening, advanced charts, real-time simulation, unrestrained access to market date, and so on.

You need to find out if the broker offers their advanced tools for free or for a price down the line. For example, several brokers offer their pro-level tools at a charge or for clients meeting certain requirements.

4. Ease of use

Because options trading platforms are so many, they each offer services streamlined for a particular group of people. Some platforms are web-based only, while some are software-based. Some are mobile-friendly, while some are optimized for a computer and some have a different interface for basic and advanced trading.

You should never use a platform that hinders you in any way. If you want a full mobile interface for advanced trading, many platforms offer this. Always visit a broker's website beforehand, both on your mobile device and desktop.

Look for quoted tutorials and tools and check out their simulated trading program.

Here are some things to consider:

- How easy can you make a trade?
- Is the mobile version of the platform enough for your needs?
- Is the design-friendly to you?
- How fast and reliable is the platform? This will be invaluable if your strategy relies on split-second trading.
- What are the charges? Is it monthly or annual? How can the charges be waived?

Bottom line

So far, you have learned that options trading can be a lonely path. But, not just that, it is a lonely path riddled with many mistakes. However, having the right knowledge of these mistakes and the right broker helps. There is a learning curve associated with trading options, every trader needs to learn as much as possible as fast as possible in order to avoid mistakes.

In the next two chapters. You will learn both basic and advanced option trading strategies.

CHAPTER SIX
Basic Option Strategies

As the saying goes; "Failing to plan is planning to fail." This is even truer in options trading. Without a clear goal and a good plan, success becomes impossible at options, unless you are really lucky.

In this chapter, we'll consider the six basic options trading strategies. How they work and the goal of each strategy. Without further ado, let's get into it.

1. Long Call

The long call is the simple strategy by which the traders buy a call option; this is otherwise known as "going long" on a call. The trader is making a bet that the stock will keep rising before the expiry.

This is the most straightforward strategy in options trading and it's a very good one because the potential profit is limitless. If the market rises, the investors stand to earn many times their investment.

For example, Pepsi Co. stocks trade at $132 per share. A trader can buy a call of a $132 strike with an expiration of 3 months at $1.5. A contract will cost $150.

In this instance, the break-even point is $133.5($132+1.5). If the stocks go beyond the break-even point at or before expiration, the trader stands to earn $100 for every dollar the stock increases above the breakeven point.

Risk/Reward: The potential profit of going long on a call is uncapped. The goal of the trader is to make as much profit as possible. More experienced traders set a cap to the profit they are expecting and they sell once the stock appreciates to a certain target.

The drawbacks of purchasing a call are that you stand to lose your investment. Although, it's possible to salvage some of the Premium by selling out the call at a cheaper rate before it expires.

Justification: Unless you are ready to lose all or part of the Premium, a long call is not a wise move. However, if you don't mind losing the Premium, it's a fantastic strategy as long as you are confident in your position regarding the underlying stock.

Your forecast needs to be positive regarding the stocks.

Investors who believe a stock is about to rise often use long calls rather than owning stocks. Because it gives them the opportunity to make a profit on the same stocks at a fraction of the cost.

2. Long Put

A long put is quite similar to a long call. However, in this instance, the trader is making a bet on the stocks' decline in the future. The trader hopes that the stock price will fall or stay flat till the expiration date.

The value of a put increases as the stock price reduces contrary to that of a call that decreases. The profit margin of a long put, however, is limited because the stock price cannot plunge below zero. But it's still a good investment as the trader can earn multiple times the initial investment.

Still using the Pepsi Co. stocks as an example; the trader can buy a contract of 4-month $132 Pepsi Co. put that is trading at $1 each. The total sum of her investment in the form of the premium will be $100 per contract.

If the stock crashes to zero before the expiry date, the trader can make as much as $13,100 in profit. But this doesn't need to happen. The break-even point is $131, after which she stands to make $100 for every dollar the stock declines beyond $131.

Risk/Reward: A long put is for traders with a bearish position on a particular stock. It's a sort of insurance policy. Should the stock ever go below the break-even point, the trader makes a profit.

But the profit is capped to the total sum of the shares at strike price minus the premium. This has a lower potential profit compared to a long call.

The downside of the long put is that the trader will lose the entire investment if the stocks appreciate. This is unless they chose to trade out the option at a loss before expiry.

Justification: Longing a put is a good strategy if you expect the stock to decline significantly before expiry. If it does, you can make a profit as long as the market price is below the break-even point.

Investors prefer this strategy to short selling their stocks. A put limits the investor's losses while the risk of short-selling stocks is uncapped.

Pertaining to this explanation. As a put owner, you must be ready to lose your premium if the market goes against you. If the stock price rises or stays flat or plummets to just above the break-even point, you will not make any profit.

3. Short Put

This strategy is the exact opposite of a long put. Here you are taking on the role of the option seller. When a trader sells a put, it is commonly referred to as "going short" on a put. You have a bullish position on the stock and you are betting that the stock price stays above the strike price at expiry. For the sale of the put, you receive a premium.

For instance, for a Pepsi Co stock trading at $132, you can write a 4 month $132 puts that sell for $1. You get paid $100 per contract. However, it is a must you buy those shares at $132 if the stock trades below the strike price.

Risk/Reward: The profit margin of shorting a put is limited to the premium you received. Even if the stocks rise a tenfold, the maximum profit you get is the premium.

However, the downside is the total value of the stocks at the strike price minus the premium. This can be a lot. If the stocks plummet to a zero, you can lose as much as $13,100 on a single put contract.

Justification: Selling puts is similar to selling insurance, traders sell it without the aim of paying out. Traders often use short puts to generate income. They are confident that the stocks will rise. So, they sell puts to other investors hoping the stocks will decline.

If the trade pans out, the trader keeps the premium and can choose to write another put.

However, as a trader, there is a need for extreme caution. Even though you are not willing to fulfill the puts, you are obligated to. If the stock falls, you can end up reaping a huge loss a hundred times the premium received.

A short put is a good strategy as long as are confident of the stocks' movement. You must have enough equity in your brokerage account to cover for the stocks before you can sell a put.

4. Covered Call

A covered call is similar to shorting a put. But it gets interesting. In a covered call, the trader selling a covered call has to own the number of underlying stocks he is writing calls for. If he is writing 5 Pepsi Co calls, he needs to own 500 Pepsi Co. shares.

Writing a call without owning the underlying stock is known as "shorting a naked call." This is the most risk intensive trade in all of the options trading. The rule is to never do this.

Owning the stock turns a risky trade into a somewhat fair trade that can generate income. This makes shorting a call safer.

Traders selling out calls are bearish on the stock, they expect the curve to stay flat or decline. So, they sell calls to investors hoping that the shares go up. If the market price finishes above the strike price before expiry, the trader is obligated to sell the stock at the strike price to the option holder.

Risk/Reward: As always with being an option writer, the maximum profit is limited to the premium received upfront; this is regardless of how great the stock price increases.

If the trade goes your way, you get to pocket the premium and you are free to write new calls or do anything you want with the shares.

The downsides aren't that easy though. You have a lot to lose in potential profit if the stock appreciates greatly during the call's time period. The shares can get called away and all you have is the premium.

But that's not all. You also have a lot to lose if the stock price crashes down. The option holder will simply allow the option to expire and you will be left with depreciated stocks.

Justification: A covered call is a popular strategy with investors for two reasons.

One, it's for those investors hoping to generate income on the stocks they have a short-term bearish position on. It's the perfect strategy for generating income with limited risk on stocks that are expected to stay flat or move slightly down before the options expiry date.

It's quite popular because if the trade pans out, the premium becomes an extra source of cash apart from dividends; especially in tax-deferred accounts.

Secondly, investors use covered calls to sell their shares at desirable strike prices they are comfortable with. For instance, you can write and sell a 2 month $220 Microsoft call, which has a current stock price of $208 at $4 each. A contract fetches you $400.

If Microsoft stock price rises to $220 or beyond in two months. The holder exercises the options and you receive a net amount of $224 per share or an amount of $220 per share plus the premium received. It's hard to go wrong with this.

However, if the stock price stays below $220 until expiration. You pocket the premium and can try the strategy again.

5. Married Put

A married put is more similar to a covered call, although it's is a little more complex. A married put is a marriage between buying a put and owning the equivalent amount of stocks the put covers.

This is the strategy used by shareholders with a long term bullish position and a short-term bearish position. It's for those who want to keep the stocks for potential profit while safeguarding their position against a decline.

For example, an investor having 500 Microsoft shares with a current market price of $208 can buy five 6-month $208 puts trading at $1 each to hedge her position. The total investment is $500.

Risk/Reward: Married puts have perplexing rewards. This is because the trader is not hoping for the stock to go down but up. If the stock appreciates, the potential profit is essentially infinite. As long as the stock price goes beyond the breakeven point of $209(strike price and premium), the trader makes a profit.

The maximum gain is simply the total stock appreciation minus the premium. If this is what happens, the trader will allow the option to expire. The option has served its purpose as insurance here.

If the stock depreciates drastically though, the trade still pans out. The trader will exercise, sell out the stocks at the strike price, and be protected from substantial loss. If the stocks go below $207, she stands to earn $500 for every dollar the stock depreciates. This is not bad for an investment of $500.

Justification: A married put is justified if you believe in the stocks' long term future but having doubts at the same time. The married put allows you to profit from an upside movement while protecting you from significant losses if the stock falls.

The only time you run into problems is when the stock stays flat on the strike price. In this instance, the option will expire worthlessly and you will lose all your investment.

Bottom line

Options will always be a risky and complex trade. However, the good news is that a trader has multitudes of strategies to choose from.

And understanding the risk and reward of every strategy is paramount. The basic strategies discussed above will help you understand what you want from each trade and the risk you are taking on.

CHAPTER SEVEN
Advanced Option Strategies

While the basic strategies are simple ways to make a profit with easily understood risks. There are many sophisticated and interesting strategies available to investors that take things up a notch. It is these strategies that make stock options an interesting topic.

In this chapter, you will learn eight advanced strategies. Hopefully, they'll teach you a thing or two on how to profit from options trading. Let's get into it.

1. Protective Collar

The first avant-garde strategy we'll consider is the protective collar. This is the developed version of a married put because it goes a further step.

An investor performing a protective collar purchases an out-of-the-money put for a stock owned while selling out an out-of-the-money call option at the same time. Both options will have the same expiration date.

This is best suited for investors having stock that has appreciated greatly since purchase. This strategy places an attractive and fixed sale price on the stock. The only downside is that they will be forced to sell the stocks it appreciated greatly, thereby relinquishing further profits. Therefore the advantage is also the disadvantage.

How it works: Imagine a trader bought some Nike shares at $50 years ago. Now, a single share is worth $98. To be on the safer side, the trader can perform a protective collar by purchasing a 2-month $93 Nike put and writing a 2-month $103 Nike call.

In this instance, the trader is protected from any price drop below $93. If that doesn't happen, though, the trader gets to keep the premium. The downside is that the trader is obligated to sell if the stock price rises above $103.

Looking on the bright side. Most traders using a protective collar are satisfied with this. This is because they have already made substantial gains on the stocks since purchase.

2. The Bear put spread

A Bear put spread is one of the two vertical strategies we'll be considering.

A vertical strategy is the simultaneous purchase of options of the same type and expiry but with different strike prices. A vertical spread mitigates risks by limiting the losses of premium but at the cost of a capped profit.

In a vertical strategy, the trader buys options at a higher strike price and sells an equal amount of options at a lower strike price. In a Bear put spread, the trade buys puts at a certain price and then writes an equivalent amount of puts at a lower strike price. This strategy corresponds with the trader having a bearish sentiment and expecting the stock price to fall.

How it works: Buying and selling put simultaneously limits the risk to the premium paid for the option.

For example, a trader may purchase a 3-month $72 puts for a stock trading at $72 at $4.5 each. At the same time, the trader can write a 3-month put with a strike price of $60 at $2 each. For a contract, the trader pays $450 while receiving $200. Thus, the total investment is $300, which is lower compared to simply going long on the put.

The break-even point for the trader will be $69. The downside of a bear put spread is that the maximum profit is capped. The trader can only ever make a maximum profit of $900, regardless of how low the stock price drops beyond the agreed strike price. Why $900?

Take a look at the breakdown:

At a stock price of $60 or below, the trader exercises his options at $72; $72 strike price multiplied by 100 shares equals $7200. But don't forget that he is obligated to pay $6000($60 strike price x 100) to the option holder of his own puts. This leaves $1200 on the table. Removing the total investment of $300 from leaves $900. Even if the stock price falls to zero, this is all the profit the trader will make.

A Bear put spread is a way to make a modest bet on a stock declining without committing in fully. Its many advantages over a long put include a cheaper price and a fixed loss. But this is at the cost of a substantial profit.

3. The Bull call spread

The other form of vertical strategy is the Bull call spread. In a bull call spread, the investor is making a bet on the stocks' rise in the future. The trader thereby pairs the purchase of a call of a lower strike price with the sale of a similar call of a higher strike price.

The bull call spread has the same upsides and downsides with the bear put spread. The long call protects the trader's portfolio from the disastrous danger of a short call. However, it similarly limits the profit margin

How it works: A trader interested in a bull call spread purchases a 3-month $70 calls for a stock trading at $70 for $5. To offset the premium paid, the trader sold a similar 3-month call at a strike price of $80 at $2.5 each. She pays $500 while receiving $250, therefore, her total investment is $250.

The breakeven point for her trade will be a stock price of $72.5(70+2.5). Ignoring commission and taxes, if she exercises at a market price of $72.5. Theoretically, she gets to recoup her total investment.

However, her profit is not unlimited like that of a long call. Her total profit can only be $750, which will be achieved at the strike price of the call she sold.

Here's the breakdown:

If she exercises at a market price of $80; she can buy 100 shares at $7000, sell them to her own option holder at $8000, thereby making an instant profit of $1000. This leaves a maximum profit of $750 when you remove the $250 paid earlier.

Her profit is technically capped at $750 because she is obligated to sell to the option holder at $8000, regardless of the market price. Even if the stocks rises to $100, the trader can only make that capped profit of $750.

A Bull call spread is advisable if you are hoping for a modest rise regarding a particular stock. It's a safer bet compared to a long put. It's also cheaper but it comes with a narrower breakeven point. So, you must be ready to risk losing your investment for a capped profit.

4. The long strangle

A long strangle is yet another sophisticated strategy that involves a double transaction. An investor carrying out a long strangle purchases a long call and a long put at the same time. With both options being out-of-the-money.

The long strangle gambles that the stock will move significantly in one direction, but the investor is unsure of which direction. Therefore the investor is making a bet in both directions and hoping that the shift will be large enough to cover the cost of the premiums.

Because this strategy uses out-of-the-money options, it is significantly cheaper compared to a long straddle; which uses at-the-money options.

The long strangle requires a large shift in either direction before it can turn in a profit.

How it works: A trader speculates on Novartis AG stock trading at $80. He goes on to buy a 4-month $90 call selling at $2.5 each and a 6-month $70 selling at $2.5 each. Both contracts cost $500.

The potential profit of a long straddle is technically infinite. The breakeven point is gotten by adding $5 to the strike price in either direction. On the call, an increase above $95($90 strike price + $5 total premium) on the stock market offers potential infinite returns.

On the put though, the maximum profit is limited to the total value of the stocks at the strike price minus the total premium. In this case, that is $6500([$70x100]-$500). As soon as the stock drops below $65, the strategy starts to turn a profit.

The major hurdle of a long strangle ensues when the stock moves but not as much as predicted. The break-even range is from $65 to $95 dollars, any movement within this range in some loss of some of the premium paid. And, if the stock price stays flat at $80, both options expire worthless, leaving behind a loss of $500.

The long strangle can be a good strategy for traders expecting a strong market shift in a direction they are not sure. It's a cheap strategy that offers potential unlimited returns. However, the risk is higher because of the wide break-even range prompted by the out-of-the-money options.

5. The long straddle

The long straddle is simply the version of a long strangle that uses at-the-money options. The trader is still in the same position, a large market shift is expected, although the direction is unclear.

So the trader purchases an at-the-money call and another at-the-money put. Both options have similar strike prices and expiration.

A long straddle offers the same upsides as a long strangle. There is an opportunity for unlimited gains if the stock rises and a massive capped gain if it falls. But because this strategy uses at-the-money options, it further complicates the risk. In that, the options are more expensive while the breakeven price range is narrowed.

How it works: Novartis AG stocks trade at $80. A 6-month $80 call is available at $5 and a 6-month $80 is available at $5 each. A trader performing a long straddle will purchase both options for a combined investment of $1000.

Unlike a long strangle that uses out-of-the-money options, the at-the-money options offer a narrower breakeven range. This will be is $70-$90 in the scenario above. Any exercise done within this will return some of the premiums.

For the call to turn a profit, the stocks need to rise above a lower $90 compared to the $95 of a long strangle.

Similarly for the put, the price only needs to drop to $70 for the trader to break even. Also, the maximum potential profit is higher at $7000([80x100]-1000).

A long straddle is a good strategy. However, the significant cost of purchasing two at-the-money options gives it a sizable drawback.

Unless the investors are sure of a massive price movement, the use of the strategy is ill-advised. This is because if the price movement is not large enough, the trader will lose some of their investment. And if the price doesn't move at all. The trader will lose 100% of the premium.

6. Long Butterfly Spread

The long butterfly spread is for advanced traders who believe the underlying stock will not move much before expiration. To carry it out, a trader has to combine a bull spread strategy with a bear spread strategy, all while using different strike prices. All the options must be for the same stock and with the same expiration date.

How it works: A trader interested in a long butterfly spread performs it by buying one in-the-money call, another out-of-the-money call, while also selling two at-the-money options.

The aim of the trader is to pocket the net gain gotten from the sale of premiums. For a stock trading at $80, a trader can get a 30-days $77 call at $3 each and 30-days $83 call at $0.5 each. While she could sell her 30-days $80 calls at $2.5 each. The trader pays $350 while earning $500 in replacement, hereby making her profit $150. This is the maximum gain that can be squeezed out of the strategy.

This maximum gain is made at the $80 strike. As the stock price moves further away from the ATM strike (either up or down) the greater the loss the seller inquires.

The maximum loss happens when the stock settles either below the lower strike call or above the higher strike call. In the instance the stock settles below the lower strike, all the options expire worthlessly and the trader is left with a depreciated stock.

If the stock settles above the higher strike, the trader is forced to sell twice the amount of shares at a considerable loss.

7. Iron Condor

In an iron condor strategy, the trader simultaneously combines a bull put spread and a bear call spread. It is designed for traders to make revenue in the form of a premium on a slowly moving stock.

How it works: It is carried out by conducting two separate trades. The first trade is the bull put spread which combines the purchase of an out-of-the-money put with the sale of another out-of-the-money put of a higher strike.

The second trade is the bear call spread which combines the sale of one out-of-the-money call with the purchase of another out-of-the-money call of a higher strike. All options are of the same underlying stock and have the same expiry date.

Usually, the calls and puts have the same spread width, hence why the strategy is labeled "condor."

Many traders owning stocks with low implied volatility prefer this strategy because of its positive probability of earning a modest amount of premium in the long-term.

However, this is an advanced strategy. With this strategy, the trader has a wider trading range to make a profit compared to a long butterfly. But the maximum profit is still limited to the premium received.

The farther away the stock price deviates from the shorts—positive deviation for the calls and negative deviation for the puts—the greater the loss inquired.

And the maximum loss is significantly higher compared to the maximum gain in the form of premium. Therefore, this strategy is suitable only for the stocks that rarely move. But even with that, there is no trade without its risks.

There is always the possibility that a trade will always end with a marginal profit.

8. Iron Butterfly

The last strategy we will cover is the iron butterfly. In this strategy, the trader similarly performs two different trades simultaneously.

The first is the purchase of an out-of-the-money call and the sale of an at-the-money call.

The second is the purchase of an out-of-the-money put and the sale of an at-the-money put. All options will be for the same stock and have the same duration.

With the sale of two at-the-money options and purchase of two out-of-the-money option, the trader makes a sizable net profit on the sale of premium. This profit is however the maximum gain.

How it works: This strategy is the hybrid of two spreads, it effectively combines an at-the-money straddle with two protective wings. The long put protects the seller from significant losses (when the stocks fall to zero). While the long call protects the seller from unlimited downsides should the stock price rise.

This is a relatively safer strategy but the downsides is that the profit is within limited margins, depending on the strike prices used. Nonetheless, investors with non-volatile stocks prefer this because of the recurrent income it can generate.

It is a safer strategy because the maximum loss only occurs when the market price either goes above the long call strike price or below the long put strike price.

Conclusion

You have now learned the eight most common advanced strategies in all of stock options trading. These strategies take trading up a notch and really shows the flexibility available to option traders. They show how beneficial options can be while also offering a glimpse into how risky they can be.

The ball is all in your court now. Throughout the course of this guide. You have learned everything a beginner is supposed to know. Surely by now, you have come to the realization that options trading can't be rushed, and neither can you rely on luck.

It's a trade that required logic and a lot of data. However, it's quite possible for anyone to make profits from options trading. You can make a profit. You just have to make sure you are trading on the right call and making the right speculations. The goal of options trading is to make consistent gains with highly calculated risk.

There is no room for luck. If you rely on luck because you have been winning with a complex strategy, a single loss can outdo all your winning. So it is vital to understand all the risks. But regardless. Options trading is a fantastic tool. You just have to use them the right way.

REFERENCES

...

James Chen, "Stock Option Definition" Feb 3, 2020. Investopedia.com Web. Accessed on 30th June 2020. https://www.investopedia.com/terms/s/stockoption.asp

Roger Wohlner, "What Stock Options are and how they work" June 5th, 2019. Wealthsimple.com. Web. Accessed on the 1st of July 2020. https://www.wealthsimple.com/en-ca/learn/what-is-a-stock-option

Fidelity trading strategy desk, "7 common mistakes in options trading" August 4th, 2019. Fidelity.com Web. Accessed on the 2nd of July 2020. https://www.fidelity.com/learning-center/investment-products/options/7-common-options-mistakes

Elvis Picardo, "Employee Stock Options." July 27, 2019. Investopedia.com. Web. Accessed on June 30th, 2020. https://www.investopedia.com/terms/e/eso.asp

Karen Rogers, "Expiration Day Mistakes to avoid with stock options." March 29, 2019. Zack's Finance. Web. Accessed on June 25th, 2020. https://finance.zacks.com/expiration-day-mistakes-avoid-options-10624.html

Ron Ianieri, "The 4 advantages of options trading." June 25th, 2019. Investopedia.com Web. Accessed on June 24th, 2020.

https://www.investopedia.com/articles/optioninvestor/06/options4advantages.asp

Charles Mackay "Extraordinary Popular Delusions and the Madness of Crowds" 1814. Accessed on 28th June 2020

Michael Molinsky, "Some Original Sources for Modern Tales of Thales - The Tales of the Olive Presses and of the Well". Accessed on 28th June 2020. https://www.maa.org/book/export/html/692721

Dana Anspach, "Understanding Your Employee Stock Options." Feb 3rd, 2020. The Balance. Web. Accessed on 29th June 2020. https://www.thebalance.com/understanding-your-employee-stock-options-2388513

Brian Burns, "A Brief History of Stock Options" 8th Sept. 2009. Thestreet.com. Web. Accessed on the 28th of June 2020. https://www.thestreet.com/opinion/a-brief-history-of-stock-options-10595277

Johnson Hur, "History of Stock Options". Bebusinessed.com Web. Accessed on 29th of June 2020 https://bebusinessed.com/history/history-stock-options/

James Chen, "Securities and Exchange Commission (SEC)" Investopedia.com. Web. May 5, 2020. Accessed on June 29, 2020. https://www.investopedia.com/terms/s/sec.asp

James Chen, "Chicago Board of Trade (CBOT)" Investopedia.com. Web. March 30, 2020. Accessed on June 29, 2020. https://www.investopedia.com/terms/c/cbot.asp

Derek Silva, "How do employee stock options work." March 24th, 2020. SmartAsset. Web. Accessed on 30th June 2020. https://smartasset.com/investing/how-do-stock-options-work

James Royal, "Option Trading Strategies for beginners." May 30, 2019. Bankrate. Web. Accessed on 1st July 2020. https://www.bankrate.com/investing/options-trading-strategies-how-to-beginners/

Mark Wolfinger, "Options trading strategy guide for 2020." Jan 7th, 2020. Stock trader. Web. Accessed on 1st July 2020. https://www.stocktrader.com/options-trading/

Lucas Downey, "10 Options strategies to know." May 29, 2020, Investopedia.com. Web. Accessed on 2nd July 2020. https://www.investopedia.com/trading/options-strategies/

James Royal, "Strategies for advanced options trading." July 5, 2017. Nerd wallet. Web. Accessed on 3rd July 2020. https://www.nerdwallet.com/blog/investing/advanced-options-trading-strategies/

Stock options for beginners

www.ingramcontent.com/pod-product-compliance
Lightning Source LLC
Chambersburg PA
CBHW071413210526
45465CB00001B/367